Changes
that
Heal
Workbook

Also by Dr. Henry Cloud and Dr. John Townsend

Boundaries

Boundaries Workbook

Boundaries audio

Boundaries video curriculum

Boundaries in Dating

Boundaries in Dating Workbook

Boundaries in Dating audio

Boundaries in Dating curriculum

Boundaries in Marriage

Boundaries in Marriage Workbook

Boundaries in Marriage audio

Boundaries in Marriage curriculum

Boundaries with Kids

Boundaries with Kids Workbook

Boundaries with Kids audio

Boundaries with Kids curriculum

How People Grow

How People Grow Workbook

How People Grow audio

How to Have That Difficult Conversation

Making Small Groups Work

Making Small Groups Work audio

Our Mothers, Ourselves

Raising Great Kids

Raising Great Kids for Parents of Preschoolers curriculum

Raising Great Kids Workbook for Parents of Preschoolers

Raising Great Kids Workbook for Parents of School-Age Children

Raising Great Kids Workbook for Parents of Teenagers

Raising Great Kids audio

Safe People

Safe People Workbook

12 "Christian" Beliefs That Can Drive You Crazy

Changes *that* Heal
WORKBOOK

Four Practical Steps to a
Happier, Healthier You

Dr. Henry Cloud

ZONDERVAN
BOOKS

ZONDERVAN BOOKS

Changes That Heal Workbook
Copyright © 1994, 2018 by Henry Cloud

Published in Grand Rapids, Michigan, by Zondervan. Zondervan is a registered trademark of The Zondervan Corporation, L.L.C., a wholly owned subsidiary of HarperCollins Christian Publishing, Inc.

Requests for information should be addressed to customercare@harpercollins.com .

Zondervan titles may be purchased in bulk for educational, business, fundraising, or sales promotional use. For information, please email SpecialMarkets@Zondervan.com.

ISBN 978-0-310-35179-5 (softcover)

Published in association with Yates & Yates, www.yates2.com.

Cover design: Faceout Studio
Interior design: Denise Froehlich

Printed in the United States of America

24 25 26 27 28 LBC 26 25 24 23 22

Contents

Introduction

This book is not designed to be read through mindlessly as you lounge in a comfortable easy chair. It does not invite merely pondering the condition of your life. Instead, it is intended to shatter any false assumptions you have about healing, uncover any cultural theologies that entrap you, correct any misunderstandings you have about God, and bring to light those dark areas of denial that exist in your life.

Furthermore, this book is not designed to resolve the debate between psychology and theology, nor does it differentiate between "emotional" problems and "spiritual" problems. Instead, based on the fact that all of our problems stem from a failure to reflect the image of God, this book calls you to rigorous self-examination through questions that will pierce your heart, motivate you to make changes in your life, and enable you to experience the healing God wants to give you.

After all, it is the Bible—God's Word—that points the way to freedom and wholeness and offers solutions for your struggle, whether it is with depression, anxiety, panic, addictions, or guilt. These solutions are based on an understanding of certain of your basic developmental tasks and in acknowledging that you—like all the rest of us—have, to some degree, failed to complete these tasks when you were growing up. Completing these tasks now will lead to changes that heal.

Let me briefly explain why. Since we have not developed the "image" of God in the vital areas of our person, we are not functioning as we were created to function. These tasks involve growing up and into the image of the One who created us. In fact, these tasks reflect the personality of God; and, if we were to cultivate them, they would greatly improve our day-to-day functioning.

The following four tasks—things that God can do but that we, his children, often have difficulty doing—are fundamental to our journey of healing:

- Bonding to others
- Separating from others
- Sorting out good and bad
- Becoming an adult

This guide is designed to help you go beyond understanding these tasks to mastering them.

As you undertake each of these four tasks, the first step is recognizing and understanding the issues surrounding each one and how your current life problems are related to them—understanding, for instance, how a problem with depression is related to the issue of isolation. The issues in your life are very much related to the people in your life, people who were important to you in the past and who are important to you in the present; how you work out these issues today will guide who is important to you in the future and how successful those relationships will be.

If you are truly to understand the issues of your life, it is crucial that you are honest with yourself about who you are and why you are that way. This kind of honesty—this agreeing with God about our faults, which the Bible calls "confession"—means understanding where we are in light of his standard. Once we understand where we are broken and where we fall short, we can work with God to reclaim those lost parts of his image and experience healing where we have been wounded.

We cannot control what has happened to us in the past, nor can we control the people in our lives now. But we can control ourselves today. We can work with God to make changes in our character and changes in how we relate to the important people in our life. These changes that we make will ultimately be changes that heal because, through them, we will be redeemed from the damage done in the past and freed to grow our undeveloped parts into his image.

As you work through these tasks, remember that it is God who will work the changes in you and bring you healing. And, since he chooses to administer that healing grace through his people, it is crucial that you do not travel this journey alone. A safe friend and/or a consistent, prayerful support group with whom you can honestly share yourself, with whom you can be vulnerable and real, who are journeying themselves in the healing process, and who are able to share what they are learning will greatly facilitate this healing process. In fact, the presence of such a community is implicit throughout the material.

Now, as you begin, let me remind you once again of the promise of Philippians 1:6: "He who began a good work in you will carry it on to completion until the day of Christ Jesus." Let these powerful words of truth—words that testify about God's love and compassion—encourage you along the way.

DR. HENRY CLOUD
NEWPORT BEACH, CALIFORNIA

How to Use This Guide

- **In community**—As you will read again and again throughout the book, God intends for us to experience his grace through his people (Rom. 12:5, 8). Our brothers and sisters in Christ are to encourage us on our journey by sharing their own story, holding us accountable as we test new behaviors, and praying for us each step along the way. We need the support of a community of people who are themselves growing. Their perspective and personal commitment to making changes that heal will strengthen us when we encounter opposition from those who disagree with the changes we make. So find a safe friend and a safe community who will be available as you work on the tasks of bonding, setting boundaries, resolving the issues of good and bad, and becoming an adult. After all, it is in healthy relationships with ourselves, other people, and God that we find healing, and it is these healthy relationships that bring us meaning, purpose, satisfaction, and fulfillment.
- **Prayerfully**—When it comes to opening our heart to God's truth, seeing ourselves for who we really are, understanding what God wants us to be in him, and changing behaviors and thought patterns that have been ours for years, it is good to remember that we don't have to do these things by ourselves. God is the One who brings healing, insight, and comfort (2 Cor. 1:3–4), and each step of the way we can turn to him in prayer, asking for guidance, understanding, courage, peace, strength, and hope when we need it. This journey of healing is, at the same time, a journey of prayer.

- **Honestly**—Hear the words of David: "You desire truth in the innermost being, . . . Search me, O God, and know my heart; try me and know my anxious thoughts; and see if there be any hurtful way in me, and lead me in the everlasting way" (Ps. 51:6; 139:23–24 NASB). This man after God's own heart knew how important it is for us to be honest with and about ourselves. And the more honest you are with yourself as you work through these lessons, the more you'll benefit from this guide. As you know from the introduction, the questions in this book call for rigorous self-examination and are designed to bring to light those dark areas of denial that exist in your life. God can use the piercing questions that follow to help free you from the past and motivate you to make the changes in your life that will enable you to experience the healing he wants to give you (John 10:10).

- **Courageously**—Change does not come easily. Freeing oneself from long-held ways of thinking and deep-seated patterns of feeling and behaving doesn't happen overnight. Leaving behind the comfortable and familiar even when it's unhealthy naturally causes nervousness and anxiety. As you begin to move toward making changes that heal, remember that you are not alone on the journey. Jesus is with you (Heb. 13:5), and he has given you his Spirit to guide, comfort, and encourage you (John 14:26).

- **Actively**—We tend to think that if we learn truth and have the right ideas in our head, we'll change, but the Bible teaches otherwise. Jesus says that "everyone who comes to me and hears my words and puts them into practice" is like a person building a house on rock (Luke 6:47–48). We are building on sand, however, if we don't put into practice what we learn. James is direct when he says, "Do not merely listen to the word, and so deceive yourselves. Do what it says" (James 1:22). Only when we continually practice what we're learning about these new behaviors based on truth will we, over time, change. So practice, practice, practice what you read here, and, with God's blessing, you will come to experience healthy relationships and the meaning, purpose, satisfaction, and fulfillment they offer.

LESSON 1

Three Ingredients
of Growth

Before We Begin

- The title of the book is *Changes That Heal*. What about this title compelled you to buy the book?
- What do you want to gain from this study? What hopes and goals do you have for yourself? What hurts do you hope to find healing for?
- What hesitations, concerns, or fears do you have as you begin this journey of healing?
- Let your hopes and goals as well as your hesitations and fears give shape to a prayer to God, the One who is an ever-present Friend, the Great Physician, and the Compassionate Healer:

God, you know the pain I carry and the scars I bear. You know, too, the hopes I have for wholeness, the dreams I have for freedom from the past, and the goals

I have for becoming more like you. As I begin this journey of healing, you also know my fears. So as I start out on this journey, God, I ask that you would give me the courage I need to look at myself, the courage to trust you, and the courage to make the changes that, with your blessing, will mean healing, freedom, and Christlikeness. I pray in Jesus' name. Amen.

Grace

Grace is the unmerited favor of God toward his people. Grace is something we have not earned and do not deserve. Grace is unconditional love and acceptance (pp. 23–25).[1]

- Describe a time when you experienced a touch of grace and how it affected you.
- Grace leads to an unbroken, uninterrupted, unearned, accepting relationship. With whom have you risked sharing your real self? What fears did you have as you developed this relationship? What feelings and thoughts have come with being known and loved anyway?
- Why is grace necessary for growing up in the image of God?
- Grace and love are the essence of God. "God is love," writes the apostle John (1 John 4:8). When have you been touched by God's love or grace, and how has his love affected you? Be specific.
- One of the primary ways God touches us with his grace is through people (1 Peter 4:10). When have you experienced God's grace through people? What is keeping you from putting yourself among God's people?
- Shame causes us to hide (p. 25). What parts of you are hidden from grace? Have you had a relationship in your life where you experienced shame rather than grace? Discuss this relationship and the scars it has left with a safe friend today.

---

1. All page numbers in this workbook refer to pages in the 2018 edition of the book, *Changes That Heal*. When no page references are given for italicized text, it usually means that these sections are additional thoughts of the author on that particular topic.

Truth

Truth is what is real. It describes how things really are. It keeps us from falling into the same patterns over and over again. But separated from grace, truth can be mean (pp. 25–28).

- In the story that opens chapter 1, why is Truth characterized as mean? Why do Truth's followers scowl and scream?
- What has been your experience of truth? Have you ever come up against the hard side of truth that gives love only if you do what is right? How did that experience affect you?
- To whom have you offered truth without grace?
- Lies we've been told about ourselves can also cause us to hide. What lies have you been told about yourself? Talk about those lies and the people who told them to you with your safe friend.
- What things have you not been truthful about? What things are you not being truthful about now?
- Jesus says, "I am the way and the truth and the life" (John 14:6). Why is truth fundamental to life—to abundant life now and to eternal life in Christ? Why is truth necessary for growing up in the image of God?

Full of Grace and Truth

In his gospel, the apostle John describes God as "full of grace and truth" (John 1:14). Grace is the relational aspect of God's character; truth is the structural aspect of his character (p. 31).

- Why do we need a God who is a God of grace as well as a God of truth?

One reason we need both grace and truth is that truth without grace is judgment (pp. 25–28).

- Everywhere Ruth turned as she was growing up, she ran into some "should" and very little acceptance. This law of sin and death took its toll on her. Have you, like Ruth's father, been judgmental and offered others truth without grace?
- Have you, like Ruth, ever experienced truth without grace? What damage has that judgment done?

We need both grace and truth because grace without truth is license (pp. 29–31).

- During his growing-up years, Sam's mother rarely disciplined him. He had few responsibilities and plenty of money. This lack of limits on his life—the lack of truth and discipline—led to a chaotic lifestyle. Have you, like Sam, ever experienced grace without truth and discipline? What were its effects?

The apostle John teaches that "the law was given through Moses; grace and truth came through Jesus Christ" (John 1:17). Failure comes through the law, and redemption through Jesus. Only through Jesus can we experience a relationship of grace with the One who is truth. Grace, when combined with truth, invites the true self, the "me" as I really am, warts and all, into relationship. It is one thing to have safety in relationships; it is quite another to be truly known and accepted in this relationship.

Remember how Jesus treated the adulterous woman in John 8:3–11? He offered her grace in the form of forgiveness and acceptance. Though realizing fully that she had sinful desires and actions, he accepted her as she was and gave her direction for the future: "Go now and leave your life of sin." These two ingredients together—acceptance and direction—bring the real self into relationship. That is the only way to healing (pp. 31–33).

- What hope for your personal life do you find in the story of Jesus and the woman caught in adultery?
- With whom have you been able to share your real self? What has that experience meant to you? If you haven't yet risked sharing your real self with God or another person, why not? What are some of the roadblocks?

When Jake entered Alcoholics Anonymous, he learned that God and others accepted him as an alcoholic, as a person helpless against his problem, and so he found hope. He also learned that when he could be himself in relationship with God and with others, healing was possible (pp. 33–34).

- When we create a false self in order to protect ourselves or to be accepted, grace and truth cannot heal us. What false self have you created in order to protect yourself or be accepted?
- What is keeping you from letting go of that false self and letting in God's grace and truth?

Grace and truth are a healing combination because they deal directly with one of the main barriers to all growth: guilt. We have emotional difficulties because we have been injured (someone has sinned against us), or we have rebelled (we have sinned), or some combination of the two. As a result, like Adam and Eve, we feel guilt (pp. 34–35).

- What events have resulted in your experience of guilt? Be specific.
- What have you done that may have caused someone to experience guilt and so withdraw from others?
- What role has the church played in your experience of guilt? Has it helped to heal you or to remain hidden? Explain.

Time

Only through a combination of grace and truth is the real Jesus present. And only when the real Jesus is present can we begin to grow into the image of our Creator. Then we really can be healed, if we have one more ingredient—time. The parable of the fig tree (Luke 13:6–9) reminds us of the importance of time to our healing and growth (pp. 36–38).

- What parts of your personality have not changed over the years?
- One response to our fruitlessness is to expect perfection and to get angry when we don't perform. At the other extreme is ignoring our fruitlessness and telling ourselves that it doesn't matter. How do you respond to your fruitlessness? Why do you think you react as you do?

When we ignore our failure to bear fruit or when we, like the man in Jesus' parable, harshly judge its absence, we end up in either grace or truth, and we do not grow. When we graft grace to truth, however, we stimulate growth. The trowel of God's truth enables us to remove the falsehood, sin, and hurt that clutter the soil of our souls. The fertilizer of love and relationship enriches the soil (pp. 36–38).

- Consider the garden of your soul. What truth do you need to face and accept? What love and relationship do you need to receive in order to grow?

The Gardener breaks up the soil, adds fertilizer, and gives the garden time to produce fruit. Time is a necessity (p. 38).

- You may have been on your own journey of healing for several months or even several years. Have you been impatient with the process? And have you appreciated the necessity of time? Share your feelings on this with others.

Redemptive Time

God created all things good. When Adam and Eve ate fruit from the tree of the knowledge of good and evil, things were no longer "all good." Adam and Eve knew evil and pain. Responding immediately to protect humankind from eternal pain, God drove Adam and Eve out of eternity into redemptive time, where we live now. Here God could fix the problem and undo the effects of the fall. He could redeem his creation and bring humankind back into eternity after it was again holy and blameless.

Think of redemptive time this way: We are sick, and God has placed us in the operating room of redemptive time. Into our veins he pumps the life-giving blood of grace and truth. During surgery, he excises evil and brings us back to a holy state. We don't know how long this surgery will last. We only know that we are expected to participate actively in it, and we don't get any anesthesia. That's why growing up into the image of God often hurts so much (pp. 38–40).

- When have you felt the pain of growing up into the image of God? Be specific about when you have felt him using circumstances in your life to mold you into his image.

God uses time in our development process. We cannot will growth; it can only come through grace, truth, and time. Even God's own Son, Jesus, rested in his timing throughout his ministry. He resisted Satan's "quick fix" offers (Luke 4) and later warned against fast growth that has no depth (Matt. 13:5–6) (pp. 40–44).

- When have you, like Stan, been surprised by growth that seemed to come from nowhere? When have you been surprised by evidence that grace and truth had been working in your life?

Good Time and Bad Time

We cannot grow when we no longer participate in life. Participation in life is often stopped by childhood trauma, poor parenting, loss, pain, and injury. Twelve-year-old Katherine became an adult when her mother died. Eight-year-old Tom decided never to have friends because relationships with his name-calling peers hurt too much (pp. 45–50).

- What part of you has been pushed outside of time and forced underground so that it no longer participates in life? Have you, for instance, stopped trusting people, stopped sharing your feelings, or stopped saying no? Have you buried your pain or chosen not to develop some talent of yours? If so, what experience caused you to do this?

- When have you tried to bring that part of yourself back into real time? What did you do? How successful were you?
- If you haven't tried to bring that part of yourself back into real time, why not? How are you going to try now?

God calls us out of the darkness of our past and into the light of experience with Jesus and his body, the church. When we are in community with God's people, time can be good time; it can transform us and develop us. But if we choose to remain isolated, God cannot use time to redeem our hurts and give us what we missed out on. In that case, time is bad time, for it is not redemptive. When we do come out of hiding, God often uses our current relationships to provide the nurturing we didn't receive as children, the mentoring we missed as school-age kids, and the companionship we needed as teenagers. He has promised to take care of us (Ps. 68:5–6) (p. 49).

- How has God provided what you missed out on growing up? How is he now using your current relationships to provide the nurturing you did not receive? Are you at all resisting God's help or the love of the people he has placed in your life? If so, how?
- It may seem as if God is not providing the nurturing you missed out on. Often we don't have because we don't ask (Matt. 7:7–11; James 4:2). What would you like to ask God to provide for you?

Because time is experience, we can influence any "past" aspect of ourselves where we missed out on development. We can reach the hurting, lonely, deprived child of our past, which is still alive within us. Just because that stage is past doesn't mean that it cannot be grown up and transformed. We can all work through the trust issues of infancy, the boundary-setting issues of toddlerhood, the forgiveness issues of young childhood, the role issues of later childhood, and the separation issues of adolescence in our present adulthood. We can all grow up again (p. 50). In grace-giving relationships, where our true selves are known, accepted, and loved, our personalities can be nurtured and redeemed in God's masterful process.

- Consider the developmental issues that can be short-circuited. Which issues— trust, boundary setting, forgiveness, roles, or separation—do you think you need to work on? In what areas do you need to grow up again?
- With whom will you work on growing up again?

Grace, Truth, and Time

License occurs when we have grace without truth, judgment when we have truth without grace, and stagnation when we have time by itself. When grace, truth, and time all come together, however, we can for the first time be loved and accepted and, through practice and experience, grow in the image of God (pp. 51–52).

Read Luke 22:31–34. What predictions about Peter—one for the near future and one for the more distant future—does Jesus make here?

What message about grace, truth, and time does Jesus' interaction with Peter offer you?

The Lord accepts us fully, knowing that we will need time and experience to work out our imperfections. We have a standing in grace that gives us freedom to face the truth over time. Facing the truth includes becoming honest about where we are, acknowledging and meeting the developmental needs of our real self, experiencing the grace of relationships, learning the truth about what God wants for us, obeying the external truth of the precepts of God, and receiving forgiveness from him, which enables us to start again when we fail. It takes time to face and live out these truths, and that's what God's redemptive time is all about.

Almighty and eternal God, as I meditate on the truths of these two chapters— the grace that is your essence, the truth of your Word, and the time it may take to experience healing—I humbly thank you for your grace, your truth, and your redemptive use of time. Help me to rest in your grace, to learn from your truth, and to trust your use of time.

You know where I need your healing touch. You know those parts of me that have been hidden away and need your nurturing; you know how much I desire and, at the same time, fear healing, wholeness, and getting closer to you. I want to trust in your love for me. I want to find hope in the truths of these two chapters. I believe, God. Help my unbelief! Help me! I pray in Jesus' name. Amen.

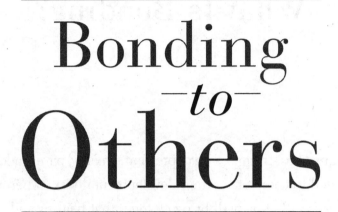

PART I

Bonding
-to-
Others

LESSON 2

What Is Bonding?

One reason many of us struggle with depression, anxiety, panic, addictions, and guilt is that we failed to complete certain developmental tasks when we were growing up. Completing those tasks now will bring changes that heal us and enable us to grow into the image of the One who created us. The first of these tasks is bonding to other people as well as to God.

What the Bible Teaches

Bonding is the ability to establish an emotional attachment to another person. It is the ability to relate to someone on the deepest level (pp. 57–58).

- Read John 15, noting especially verses 5, 6, and 12. What attachments does Jesus emphasize here?
- The Bible clearly reveals how strongly God feels about the importance of relationships. What do the following passages teach about the experience of being in relationship with fellow believers?

- Ephesians 4:16
- Ephesians 3:17–21
- Colossians 3:14 (NASB)
- 1 John 4:20–21
- Romans 15:1–7

Our need to bond is strong, and a failure to bond is disastrous for our well-being, because God is a relational being who created a relational universe. At the foundation of every living thing is the idea of relationship. Everything that is alive relates to something else (pp. 58–59).

- What do the following verses teach about God and the fact that he does not exist alone but in relationship?
  - John 14:20
  - John 17:20–23
- What do the following truths about God's character suggest about relationships?
  - 1 John 4:16
  - 1 John 4:7

Living in relationship, or bonding, is the foundation of God's nature. Since we are created in his image, relationship is our most fundamental need. Without attachment to God and others, we can't be our true selves. We can't be truly human. This truth also helps us understand why love is the highest ethic. God's law is a structure, or a blueprint, for loving. The law is the way that love is to be lived out.

What the Past Taught Me

Failure to bond in the past interferes with bonding in the present. People who never develop an emotional bond to anyone—people who are disconnected—often fear that others hate them and will hurt them. Take a few minutes to look back at your past, so that you can remember what was good in order to re-create those patterns, and recognize what was bad in order to avoid those patterns (pp. 63–66).

- With whom have you had a good bonding relationship in the past? What were the ingredients of that relationship?
- Who hurt your ability to bond and trust? What did that person/those people do? Which personality traits were hurtful to you?
- What inner convictions did you develop about yourself and others as a result of these hurtful attachments? What feelings did you develop about relationships in general?
- Have you been able to forgive the people who hurt you? If not, what is blocking you from forgiveness? Are you waiting for people to apologize or change? Do you want revenge? Do you feel angry that no one has ever listened to you or believed you? If you cannot forgive, does that fact give you a sense of power?
- Have you been able to realize that God accepts and loves you even though others have hurt you and labeled you "bad"? What keeps you from embracing that truth? (Possible barriers include the inability to be vulnerable and a distorted view of yourself, of others, or of God. If you have never shared those "bad" sides with anyone and been accepted, you may have a more difficult time believing God accepts you.)
- What parts of your bonding self (your ability, for instance, to be vulnerable, to express feelings, to share needs, or to reveal weaknesses) did you bury as a result of bad bonds from the past? Are these still buried, and if so, why?
- Where have you hurt someone else's ability to bond? Have you asked for forgiveness?

Our emotional well-being depends on the status of our heart, and the status of our heart depends on the depth of our bonds with others and with God. The Bible said this long ago (Prov. 14:30), and science is proving it today (pp. 66–67).

- Review Kyle's story. Once he opened up to a few men he trusted and shared with them his problems and concerns, he began to make connections. These attachments began to provide him comfort. Over time this comfort came to live inside him, and he discovered that he could feel loved wherever he was. Has your story been similar to Kyle's? How? Where do you think you are on your journey toward healthy bonding with other people?

In one of his last counseling sessions, Kyle observed, "I didn't know how God works. He had to take me through experiences of emotional connection with others to get me out of my pain. I wish he had done it an easier way." If you didn't bond in your original family, however, there often is no easier way. Sadly, sometimes even our church family can make the way out of our pain even more difficult (pp. 67–70).

- If you feel the church has added to your pain, remember God's truth about the value of relationships, acknowledge how you have been hurt by fellow believers, and forgive them. What do the following passages reveal about the importance of love and attachment?
  - 1 John 3:14
  - Galatians 6:2
  - Matthew 12:7

The Benefits of Attachment

Nothing is further away from the heart of God than a theology divorced from love—from a compassionate, faithful, and loyal love that imparts to the loved one a sense of belonging and attachment. People who feel attached to God find in that attachment a good basis for morality, an increased ability to handle stress, and meaning for their accomplishments in life.

A Basis for Morality

The Bible talks about a morality based on love, not on principles or rules. According to the apostle Paul, the commandments are summed up in this one rule: "'Love your neighbor as yourself.' Love does no harm to a neighbor. Therefore love is the fulfillment of the law" (Rom. 13:9–10). Since we often do what we know is wrong, rules rarely keep us in line. Love does a much better job of keeping us moral. It is the absolute rule and the absolute law (pp. 70–71).

- Explain, giving examples, why love and relationship with God are a surer foundation for morality than principles or rules.
- Describe a time when thinking about how you might hurt someone you love kept you moral.
- Describe a time when thinking about how you might hurt God, who is love, kept you moral.

An Ability to Handle Stress

When people have good friends to support them, they can handle stressful situations more easily. Bonds of love with other people and with God can bring us through dark and difficult days (John 16:33) (pp. 71–72).

- What do the following verses teach us about how to help one another handle stress?
  - Galatians 6:2
  - 1 Thessalonians 5:14
  - Ecclesiastes 4:9–12
- Describe a time when having a good friend enabled you to handle a stressful situation. Be specific about the circumstances.
- Right now, who needs your help? To whom can you offer encouragement, help, or patience? Whose burden can you help bear?
- Often our fear of needing someone keeps us from forming deep attachments with people. As a result, we find ourselves alone when life gets tough. How easy is it for you to ask someone for help, to confide your weaknesses, to need someone? Why do you hesitate to take these steps?

- If we have never let ourselves need someone, we may also struggle with letting ourselves need God. To what degree have you struggled to let yourself need God? Comment on why you have or haven't struggled.

Meaning for Accomplishments

Bonded people are able to tolerate time alone and use it constructively because, for them, being alone does not mean that they are isolated. Not afraid of being alone, these people can accomplish many things (p. 72).

- Are you or have you ever been uncomfortable being alone? What do you think is the root of that discomfort?

Bonded people also know the real reason for work. They do not work to pile up possessions or run away from pain. They work for the family of humanity. Their work is their service to God (pp. 72–73).

- What work do you do? Why do you work?
- How do you serve God and his people through your work? Or how could you begin to serve him through the work you are now doing?

In addition to providing a good basis for morality, an increased ability to handle stress, and meaning for our accomplishments, bonding also fuels the rest of our development. Learning how to bond fosters the ability to attach to others and enables us to develop in all the ways God designed.

God, I thank you that you are a relational God and that you have designed me to be in relationship with you and with others. God, you know why that kind of relationship is hard for me. You know the experiences that keep me from bonding. I know what your Word teaches about love, and I am aware of the great benefits that come when we human beings are able to bond with one another and with you.

Please use what I am learning to free me from those events in the past that keep me from attaching to you and to other people the way I want to. I pray in Jesus' name. Amen.

LESSON 3

When We Fail to Bond

The past allows us to gain insight, forgive ourselves and others, learn where our distorted thinking came from, and express our hurt. But archaeology never built a new building, and the focus of this healing process is to build something new. So, before we can work on learning how to bond, we must take a closer look at some of the disastrous results of our failure to bond.

Three Stages of Isolation

When we don't make emotional attachments to God or other people, we live in a state of perpetual hunger. We have a crying need that's not being met. As a result, we go through three stages of isolation.

The first stage we go through is protest. We feel sad and angry, and we protest our lack of relationship. If this isolation continues too long, we move into the second stage: depression and despair. Our hope that our needs will be met begins to wilt. If depression and despair continue long enough, the third stage, detachment, sets in. When we reach this stage, we are out of touch with both our own need for others and with the outside world (pp. 74–75).

- Which stages have you experienced? When have you protested your lack of relationship with God? With others? When have you felt depressed and despairing about being out of relationship with God? With other people? With whom? Have you ever experienced deadening detachment, and if so, when?
- Which stage, if any, are you in now? Are you feeling sad and angry about your isolation? Are you depressed and despairing about your aloneness? Or are you emotionally dead and detached from your need for others and from the outside world?

As painful as our becoming aware of this isolation is, it is a good thing, for it points to a vital need. We realize that we need God. In fact, our needs *drive* us to God (Matt. 5:6).

Symptoms of Failure to Bond

To fully understand the isolation you or people you know may be experiencing, consider some of the common symptoms of isolation, symptoms that often cover up the real problem, which is lack of relationship. Pages 75–83 discuss thirteen of these symptoms.

- As you read through the list of symptoms below, place a check mark next to any you've experienced. Then write down any words or phrases from the text that describe your experience, help you better understand what is going on in your life, or give you hope about moving away from isolation toward healthy bonds with God and other people.
  - Depression
  - Feelings of meaninglessness
  - Feelings of badness and guilt
  - Addiction
  - Distorted thinking
  - Emptiness
  - Sadness

- Fears of intimacy
- Feelings of unreality
- Panic
- Rage
- Excessive caretaking
- Fantasy

- What has this list of symptoms shown you about yourself? Have you been trying to manage symptoms (depression, emptiness, panic, etc.) rather than dealing with the root of the problem (failure to bond)? Explain.

Barriers to Bonding

If bonding to others can help us cure so many awful maladies, why don't we just do it? Oh, if it were that easy! Because of the fall, a whole host of problems renders us human beings isolated and unable to attach to God and one another (pp. 83–84).

Past Injury

If we were blessed with loving caretakers who met our needs when we were young, we develop our "trust muscle" and begin to perceive the world as a trustworthy place. We love because our parents first loved us; we love because God first loved us (1 John 4:19). If our needs were not met—if we were neglected, abandoned, beaten, abused, criticized, hated, or resented for existing—then our very ability to trust and be vulnerable is injured (p. 84).

- What did your caretakers teach you about the world?
- What did your caretakers teach you about God? Consider what they modeled as well as what they did or did not say.
- When you were young, what love did you reject? Why?
- If you are a parent, what are you teaching your children about the world? What is your parenting teaching your children about their heavenly Father?

- When have you injured someone and perhaps affected that person's mental map of the world and understanding about relationships? Have you apologized and asked forgiveness?

Distorted Thinking

Some of our ideas about ourselves, other people, and God are like outdated maps. Although they may have seemed accurate at one time, they no longer are. But since we don't have the knowledge or the experience to update them, we still use them as we try to find our way through life, even though they interfere with our efforts to bond with God and with one another (pp. 85–90).

- Place a check mark next to any of the following ideas that have taken up residence in your heart and mind.
  - "I am bad."
  - "I am unlovable."
  - "Something about me scares people away."
  - "My sins are worse than other people's sins."
  - "I don't deserve love."
  - "My neediness will overwhelm anyone."
  - "My need for others is not valid."
  - "My feelings will overwhelm anyone."
  - "No one is trustworthy."
  - "People will always leave me."
  - "People are mean and critical."
  - "People will disapprove of me."
  - "People will control me."
  - "People are faking their care."
  - "God doesn't really love me."
  - "God doesn't care about the way I feel. He just wants me to be good."
  - "God just wants 'good Christians.' "

- ◉ "God gets angry at me."
- ◉ "God doesn't hear me."
- ◉ "God doesn't answer prayer."
- ◉ "God will control me and take away my freedom."
- ◉ "God won't forgive me for . . ."
- What experiences gave you these distortions?
- What are you doing to counter these experiences and the resulting distortions?
- As you review the descriptions of these distorted thoughts, where do you find hope in the explanations of these inaccurate ideas?

Perhaps you've been told just to "change your thinking." This is not an easy task because we're talking about something deeper than thinking. We're talking about convictions that are held in our heart. We form our view of relationships long before we have the capacity to reason with our minds. That is why no real and deep change occurs outside of relationship and trust. If God has given you opportunity for good relationships, then you must face your distortions of the truth and bring your real self into attachment with others. Humble yourself and risk being vulnerable. God promises to help you with the task (Ps. 139:23–24; James 4:9–10) (p. 91).

- Who is available to you now that you are not connecting with? What is holding you back from entering that relationship?

Defense Mechanisms

In addition to the injuries to our "trust muscle" and the distortions of God, ourselves, and others that interfere with our bonding, we also have built up a wall of defense mechanisms against relationship (described on pp. 91–95).

- Which of the following psychological coats are you wearing to protect yourself from the hurtful cold even though you are in a land ripe with possibilities of warm relationships?

- With whom do you currently have a negative bond? Why are you staying in that relationship as it is rather than changing it? What elements of the connection are hurting you and leaving you isolated?
- How does this negative bond reinforce your distortions about yourself and the rest of the world? How is that relationship reinforcing the hurts you have experienced and your defense mechanisms?

Learning God's Ways

Past injuries, distorted thinking, and defense mechanisms are direct results of the fall; everyone has them to differing degrees. The Bible addresses all three of these directly, giving us advice on how to get past them (pp. 95–99).

Past Injuries

Early developmental injuries take time to heal. In 1 Thessalonians 5:14, Paul urges us to "encourage the disheartened, help the weak, be patient with everyone," including ourselves and those we know who are feeling the pain from past injuries (p. 95).

- To what wounded hearts can you offer encouragement and patience as they seek to enter into relationship with you?
- Whom has God placed in your life to offer you encouragement and patience? Describe the relationship being offered you. Are you showing your real self to this person who can give you grace? Are you letting yourself receive God's touch of grace through this person?

Distorted Thinking

According to Jesus, sometimes we live according to the "tradition of the elders" or "merely human rules" instead of the ways of God (Matt. 15:1–9). Unspoken family rules may lead us to living in direct contradiction with God's rules (pp. 95–98).

- Write out the ten relational commandments of the family that you grew up in.
- Have you renounced the theology of your dysfunctional family reflected in the commandments you just outlined? If so, how have they reacted? If not, why not?

Jesus knows that if our loved ones do not hold to God's values, conflict with them may come (Matt. 10:34–37). We should not turn against these friends or relatives who do not adhere to God's ways of love. We must, however, see them as enemies of our souls and seek out people who can lead us toward the image of God.

Defense Mechanisms

Although we once used various defense mechanisms to protect ourselves from getting hurt, they don't serve us well today.

- What are you doing to shed your defense mechanisms? When, for example, will you stop hiding your need for others behind busyness or workaholism? What are you substituting for a wholesome relationship in your life? What are you doing to step out of your denial or projection and to act on your own need for others and your desire for relationships?
- Whose love are you devaluing as it is being offered to you? Why won't you let yourself accept it and respond to it as evidence of God's grace?
- How did you become aware of your reaction formation—your tendency to do the exact opposite of what you want to do in a relationship? What are you doing to counter that tendency?
- Whom do you have in your life who knows the defenses you tend to use and can call you on them when you do?

Despite the injuries you sustained in the past, the distorted thinking that resulted, and the defense mechanisms you developed, you may nevertheless have been blessed with some experiences of healthy bonding. You should examine your relationships to see if they are helping you grow in the image of God. Saying no to bad relationships and yes to good ones may be difficult, but the psalmist assures us that God can cut us free from the cords of the wicked (Ps. 129:1–4). Then we can open wide our hearts to those who walk in the ways of the Lord (pp. 98–99).

- With whom do you now have a healthy relationship? What elements have helped create this bond? How can you increase those elements (i.e., be more vulnerable, take more risks, be more open about more of your needs)?
- Who is showing his/her real self to you? What are you doing to respond with grace to that vulnerability?
- If you believe that time is an element of growth, how much time each week do you invest in creating healthy attachments? If you devote little time, why?

God, you know how isolated I have felt, and you know the symptoms of isolation that I wrestle with. You know, too, the injuries I've sustained in the past, the distorted thinking that weighs me down, and the defense mechanisms that interfere with relationships. Thank you for bringing healing in time and through people. Be with me as I learn to trust, to open up, and to be vulnerable and real with people who know you and walk in your ways. And, when people open up to me, help me to give to them what I so long to have myself. I pray in Jesus' name. Amen.

LESSON 4

Learning to Bond

Learning to bond when you missed out the first time around won't happen overnight. Making human connections when you grew up without them takes a good dose of grace, truth, and time. In this lesson, we'll look at some skills that will start you on the long road to making changes that heal.

Helpful Skills

Realize the Need

Acknowledging a deep, personal need for attachment is critical, for that's where God and others can meet you. Only from a humble place of need can you receive and be filled (Matt. 5:3). This may be difficult for you, since you may have grown up in a family where closeness was not valued, or you may have been injured to the point where you have forgotten how to bond (p. 101).

- What does Paul say about attachment in 1 Corinthians 12:12–27 (note especially verses 21, 26, and 27)?

- What things have happened in your past that have made you reluctant to acknowledge your need for relationship?
- In a brief prayer right now, acknowledge before God your need for him and your need for people. Share with him your fears as you begin working to develop skills for bonding.

Move Toward Others

It is wonderful when others move toward you and seek out your heart, for that is what God does. But often other people cannot see what you need or how emotionally isolated you are. That's when you need to actively reach out for help and support (Matt. 7:7) (p. 101).

- As you look "out there," who is available and what concrete steps are you going to take to increase your relationship with those persons?
- What already structured situations can you take advantage of? That is, what are some available support groups, prayer and sharing groups, group therapies, or counselors you can investigate that will help you move ahead?
- How will you allow God to be a part of ending your isolation?

Be Vulnerable

You can move toward others, get socially involved, and have relationships, but still feel isolated. Your isolation may stem from an inability or unwillingness to be open and vulnerable, an inability to show your real self to others.

- Being vulnerable at a social level may seem too threatening at first. Who is a safe person to whom you can, one-on-one, show your real self? With whom will you share your plan to end your isolation and get review and feedback from as you put your plan into action?
- Take a few minutes to think through how you will tell that person the hurt and isolation you feel. Write down the words you will use to admit that you need support and help. Now contact that person and schedule a time to get together to talk.

Challenge Distorted Thinking about Yourself, Others, and God

Distorted thinking causes you to repeat what happened in the past. Thus, you need to challenge the distortions that keep you in bondage. Sometimes they are so much a part of our reality that we don't even recognize them for what they are. Remember, though, that the Lord has promised to reveal the truth to you and has sent his Spirit to help (John 14:6; 16:13) (p. 102).

- In what specific ways are you going to challenge your distorted thinking when those old ideas keep running through your mind? What concrete things will you do to overcome the barriers to relationships that you've developed through the years?
- What difficulties do you envision encountering as you begin to challenge your isolation? How are you going to handle these when they arise?

Take Risks

As people and God call to you to enter into relationships, your distorted thinking and your resistance to take a risk may keep you from responding. But you have a responsibility to open the door when you hear a knock and a voice calling from outside (Rev. 3:20). It is difficult but essential to healthy bonding that you allow yourself to risk getting hurt again (p. 102).

- Sometimes we cling to negative attachments because they're better than no attachments at all. Letting go of them is one risk you'll need to take. What negative attachments of "truth without grace" or "grace without truth" (see chapter 1) do you need to either change or avoid in order to grow?
- Write out Jesus' invitation in Revelation 3:20 and insert your name. Even though you may have invited him in for salvation, what about his abiding in you?
- Who in your life may be knocking on the door, wanting to enter into relationship with you? What's keeping you from opening the door? What specifically will you do to overcome those obstacles?
- Who in your life needs you to knock on his/her door and enter into relationship with that person? What's keeping you from knocking on the door? What specifically will you do to overcome those obstacles?

Allow Dependent Feelings

Whenever you begin to allow someone to matter to your isolated heart, uncomfortable needy and dependent feelings surface. These are the beginnings of a softening heart (pp. 102–3).

- What are you going to do when these uncomfortable feelings arise?

Recognize Defenses

You need to recognize your own particular defenses against attachment. Try to see the old familiar patterns when they arise, take responsibility for them, and call on the Holy Spirit to empower you to resist them (Eph. 3:16) (p. 103).

- Review the list of defense mechanisms on pages 91–95. Which ones are you aware of falling into?
- What are you going to do if you find yourself using these defenses again?

Become Comfortable with Anger

The angry self is an aspect of personhood that many people prefer to leave "unbonded." They believe it is an unlovable aspect of who they are (p. 103).

- What does Ephesians 4:26 mean to you?
- What did you learn about anger in the family you grew up in?
- Remember that it is natural to feel angry toward people you need. The more you can feel comfortable with angry feelings toward "good" people, the more you can integrate those feelings into a relationship and not spoil it. Who in your life has modeled a positive way of dealing with anger? How?
- How would you like someone who is angry at you to deal with his/her anger?
- What does your answer to the preceding question suggest to you about how you can deal with your anger toward another person?

Pray and Meditate

God is the one who brings healing; we don't heal ourselves. Therefore it is only right that we pray as we take steps toward the changes that heal (pp. 103–4).

- Pray along with David his prayer in Psalm 139:23–24. Ask God to unravel the problems in your ability to make attachments to others and to him.

> Search me, God, and know my heart;
> test me and know my anxious thoughts.
> See if there is any offensive way in me,
> and lead me in the way everlasting.

- What hope do other verses in God's Word give you for your journey toward healthy bonds with him and his people? See, for instance, Deuteronomy 31:8; Psalm 46:1–2; and Zephaniah 3:17.

Be Empathic

Empathy is the ability to share in another's emotions, thoughts, or feelings. We are commanded in Scripture to enter into one another's joy and sorrow (Rom. 12:15).

- When have you identified with a struggler and found yourself more in touch with your own hurt and loneliness?
- Who in your life right now needs an empathetic friend? Don't be afraid to draw alongside that person.

Rely on the Holy Spirit

The Holy Spirit empowers you to change and come out from the bondage of your old ways of being. Rely on him to help you make the changes that heal, to free you from the death grip of your old defenses, and to give you the courage to take the first steps to attach to others, for he is able (Eph. 3:20) (p. 104).

- What are you going to do when your distorted thought patterns and your old defenses arise?

Say Yes to Life

The task of bonding to others and to God is one of saying yes to life. Be sure to say yes when God and other people invite you to connect with them (pp. 104–5).

- Are you saying no to relationships? Are you avoiding intimacy and making excuses? Are you staying too busy to accept invitations? Are you hiding behind defense mechanisms? Are you keeping your distance rather than empathizing with others in their hurts? Even in safe contexts, do you always answer "How are you doing?" with "Fine"?
- What are you going to do to set aside the time you need to encourage bonding with others? What changes in your schedule and lifestyle will you make?

Remember the story of Tara. Isolated among an army of friends and filled with a black depression, she had tried to end her life. Her battle was not an easy one. Like a terminally ill patient, she literally had to fight for her life. Someday, however, she will face her Savior and be proud that she "fought the good fight," the one of love, and regained the lost "image of God" caused by the fall and her family background. Tara no longer lives in an earthly hell of isolation—and you don't need to either. Instead, Tara lives in the "heaven on earth" of intimate, loving relationships—and so can you (pp. 55–57, 105–6).

God, I'm glad that I am not alone in this journey. The fear of trying to master the skills I need for healthy relationships is as overwhelming as my pain. May I sense your presence and draw strength from you as I move toward others and risk letting myself be vulnerable. Holy Spirit, help me overcome my distorted thinking and familiar defenses. Help me feel comfortable with my dependence, with my anger, and with a heart that is soft enough to let myself feel another's pain. Enable me, God, to say yes to you, to the people you put in my life, and to life itself. I pray in Jesus' name. Amen.

PART 2

Separating *from* Others

LESSON 5

Understanding Boundaries

In a psychological sense, boundaries are the realization of our own person apart from others. This sense of separateness forms the basis of our personal identity. It says what we are and what we are not, what we will choose and what we will not choose, what we will endure and what we will not endure, what we will feel and what we will not feel, what we like and what we do not like, and what we want and what we do not want. Boundaries, in short, define us (p. 92).

The Biblical Basis for Boundaries

Remember the story of Stephen? He had no limits on others' control of him, no sense of personal boundaries and space, and very little of what the Bible calls "will" (pp. 109–11).

- Can you relate to Stephen? Describe a time when you kept saying yes to other people, and yet felt resentful doing so.
- Read through the following symptoms of a person who has a problem establishing and keeping boundaries. Place a check mark next to the statements that could describe you.

- You can't choose what you want to do apart from what others want you to do.
- You can't say no because you feel obliged and compelled to serve others.
- You feel responsible for other people so you don't take responsibility for your own life.
- Your lack of limits has led to chaos, resentment, panic, and/or depression.
- You've suffered physical and emotional abuse as a result of your lack of boundaries.
- You act as though you have the power to make someone feel bad or happy or angry.

If you can identify with these symptoms, you may have a problem with establishing and keeping boundaries. God created you in his image to have boundaries. Although God is a bonded person (the Father, Son, and Holy Spirit are always connected), he has diversity within this unity. The Father, Son, and Holy Spirit are each distinct, separate Persons with boundaries between them. They are not "fused" in such a way that they lose their individual identity. They each have their own talents, responsibilities, wills, and personalities.

Created in God's image, we human beings are separate from one another. We have distinct personalities, wills, talents, and responsibilities. This separateness is an important aspect of human identity. We are to be connected to others without losing our own identity and individuality. We are to master the art of "being me without the fear of being rejected by you" (pp. 112–13).

- Who has helped you become more the person you feel God designed you to be? What qualities of that relationship encouraged your personal sense of identity?
- With whom in the past were you able to discover and keep your boundaries? What qualities of that relationship supported your boundaries?

When we think of relationship, we think of love. When we think of boundaries, we think of limits. Boundaries give us a sense of what is part of us and what is not part of us, what we will allow and what we won't allow, what we will choose to do and what we will choose not to do. We see God doing this over and over again in the Bible (pp. 113–14).

- How does God define himself in the following statements?
  - Genesis 6:18
  - Genesis 17:1
  - Exodus 22:27
  - Proverbs 6:16–19
  - Isaiah 60:16
  - Isaiah 61:8
  - Ezekiel 39:26

To help us understand who God is, biblical writers name what things the Lord loves and hates, what he wants and does not want, what he chooses, what he wills, what he thinks about things, and what he does. We define ourselves in much the same way. Let's take an inventory of ten key areas to see how well you have defined your boundaries (pp. 116–34).

- *Your Physical Appearance*—Your body is a temple of the Holy Spirit (1 Cor. 6:19–20). What do you do to let good things in and keep bad things out of your body? Have you allowed others to violate your body? What do you do to take care of your body? What do you do that does more harm than good to your body?
- *Your Attitudes*—The Bible is clear about God's attitudes toward things (see, for example, the Ten Commandments in Ex. 20:1–17), and God himself tells us that if our attitudes are his attitudes, our way will be prosperous (Josh. 1:8). How well do your attitudes and beliefs line up with God's attitudes? Which of your attitudes and beliefs do you need to analyze and make sure are yours? Where are you taking responsibility for the attitudes or beliefs of other people? Own and state your attitudes.
- *Your Feelings*—In the parable of Mark 7:21–22, Jesus calls us to take responsibility for our own feelings. Are you disowning certain feelings and ignoring your responsibility for them? Which ones, and why?

- *Your Behavior*—Like our Creator, we are to take responsibility for what we do. To help us do so and to give us a sense of control and an element of power over our lives, God has set up the law of sowing and reaping (Prov. 4:26; 10:4; Gal. 6:7–8). To own our behavior, to admit it, to recognize it, to acknowledge it, in short, to take responsibility for it, is an important aspect of knowing our boundaries. When is it hard for you to take responsibility for your actions? Why? When is it hard for you not to take responsibility for other people's actions? Why?

- *Your Thoughts*—God calls us to love him with all our minds (Mark 12:30) and to take captive and evaluate every thought we have (2 Cor. 10:5). Our distorted thoughts need to be evaluated in light of his truth. What distorted thinking do you need to challenge? What passing thoughts do you need to look at more closely?

- What assumptions about other people's thinking are interfering with your relationships with them or with how you are living your life? In what contexts do you struggle to think your own thoughts?

- *Your Abilities*—God has given each of us certain talents and abilities, and he holds us responsible for developing them (1 Cor. 12:7–11, 27–28; 1 Peter 4:10). When have other people's wishes or expectations kept you from developing your own talents and abilities? What God-given talents and abilities have you nurtured? How has doing so helped you define who you are?

- *Your Desires*—God has given us many desires; others we have chosen for ourselves. Both can be good, but some of them are not. God calls us to own all of our wants and desires, for he is at work in them (Phil. 2:12–13). Discuss a time when God helped you differentiate between a good desire and a bad one.

- When have you struggled to acknowledge or own your desires? Why? How are your desires and wants helping you reach your goals in life?

- How does it feel to try to make a decision with someone who doesn't own his/her desires and answers your questions with "I don't care" or "You choose"?

- *Your Choices*—To make and own our choices, we must be aware of all the aspects of ourselves that go into any decision. We must also be aware that we are making a choice about almost everything we do, and we need to take responsibility for the feelings that our choices leave us with (2 Cor. 9:7). When in your life did you learn that not making a choice is making a choice? What things do you tend to do because you feel you "have to"? What things do you tend to do because you can't say no? What areas of your life do you complain about rather than trying to remedy?

- *Your Limits*—We all possess a finite amount of ability, time, money, energy, and so on. Many people, however, don't take responsibility for their limits and over-extend themselves. Others have limits that are too narrow (2 Cor. 9:6). Which limits do you tend to overextend—your time, money, energy, ability, emotions, or something else? Where are your limits too narrow? And where do you need to be limiting other people's demands on you?

- *Negative Assertions*—God asserts his identity by saying who he is and who he is not, and we are to do the same. Like the son who at first refused to work in the vineyard, we need to say what we are not (Matt. 21:28–31). What are some negative assertions that help define who you are? What are some behaviors, attitudes, abilities, choices, and limits that are not you?

- When have you, unlike Sandy, been able to not do something you didn't want to do and taken responsibility for the consequences (p. 134)? How did you feel? What did you learn?

- Review what you've noted about your body, attitudes, feelings, behavior, thoughts, abilities, desires, choices, limits, and negative assertions. Which of these areas do you need to work on in order to form proper boundaries?

Developing Boundaries

Perhaps you have noticed that you don't have clearly defined boundaries for yourself. Maybe the reason for that has to do with the bonding you have or have not done. Bonding must always precede separateness and the successful establishment of boundaries. If we cannot attach, then separateness—setting boundaries—has no meaning. We need to be "rooted and grounded in love" (Eph. 3:17 NASB) if we are to find the safety necessary to venture out in separateness (pp. 137–40).

- What did you learn in part 1 of this workbook about how well bonded you were as a child and how well bonded you are with people today?

- How has your bonding or struggle to bond affected your ability to set boundaries for yourself? Do you need others so much that, because of fears of isolation, you are often afraid to set boundaries? In other words, what connection do you see between the bonding you have or haven't done and the boundaries you are able or unable to set and maintain?

- After a child's first year of bonding and attachment, the process of separateness begins, and boundaries begin to develop. Are your boundaries confused because you were not allowed to own your feelings, thoughts, and behaviors? Or are your boundaries not limited enough, so that you tend to act as though you are the only one who matters? As a result, have you become, respectively, overly responsible or not as responsible as you should be?

- From the second year of life onward—through kindergarten, elementary school, adolescence, college, and beyond—bonding and separateness must work hand in hand. Think about your growth. Through the years, how have you come to own more and more things within your personal boundaries? Where have you succeeded in becoming a separate person from the people you are bonded to? With whom are you able to maintain your boundaries? Why?

As we go through life, we learn how to stay in relationship as well as how to be a separate person from the people we are bonded to. Balancing bonding and separateness enables us to lead full, productive lives and be relational people.

Boundaries: Key to Love, Freedom, and Responsibility

Ownership is crucial in creating boundaries. We need to own our thoughts, feelings, attitudes, behaviors, desires, and choices if we are to develop a true sense of responsibility for who we are. This ownership also enables us to recognize where we might be tempted to own other people's thoughts, feelings, attitudes, behaviors, desires, and choices and so violate their boundaries (pp. 140–41).

- When have you, like Sandy, tried to own what belongs to others (her mother's disappointment and anger if she chose to spend Thanksgiving with her friends)? What does Proverbs 19:19 say about what happens when you try to own someone else's anger?

It is easy to say that we love others but difficult to allow them the freedom inherent in love. But love cannot exist without freedom, and freedom cannot exist without responsibility. We must own and take responsibility for what is ours, and that includes admitting our disappointment if we do not get everything we want from another person. The disappointment that comes when our loved ones exercise their freedom is our responsibility (pp. 141–42).

- When have you, like Sandy's mother, tried to blame someone else for the pain, disappointment, or anger you were feeling rather than taking responsibility and dealing with your feelings? In what relationship are you doing so now? Can you identify with the anger of the mother in this passage? Read Matthew 20:13–15.
- Are you waiting for someone else to change rather than taking responsibility for the circumstances of your own life and acting to change them? If so, describe a situation in which you have been doing that.

When other people's freedom leads them to sin against us, it is our responsibility to deal with the pain we feel. We need to go through the appropriate blaming stage. After all, part of forgiveness is to call sin, sin. We must confess how we have been sinned against in order to forgive, but then we must begin to take responsibility for the mess that someone else's sin has left us in. Our situation is our property and we must own it—we must deal with our feelings, attitudes, and behaviors—if we are to get unstuck. And as we deal with them, we'll be learning to set boundaries so that we can avoid similar pain in the future.

- Have you been able to forgive those who hurt your sense of boundaries (Luke 6:37)? Have you called what they did to you "sin" and let them be responsible for it? Or are you taking responsibility for what is not yours before God and feeling guilt that does not belong to you?
- How is unforgiveness a chain that is binding you to people who have crossed your boundaries? What can you do to let go?

God, you made me a unique person, different from everyone else you have made; yet sometimes I'm not sure how well I know myself. I've realized that I'm not clear about my boundaries—about my attitudes, feelings, behavior, thoughts, abilities, desires, choices, and limits. Help me get to know myself.

And, God, I ask you to heal the hurts that have come because I haven't known or set any boundaries. Please repair those boundaries that I've let other people overrun and help me establish boundaries where there haven't been any strong ones before.

Give me, too, Lord, the courage to accept responsibility for my feelings and to extend forgiveness to those I love rather than to merely blame and complain about the way life is. May I offer to those I love freedom within that love, and may I discover the safety and the freedom that come with clearly defined boundaries. I pray in Jesus' name. Amen.

LESSON 6

Crossing Over Boundaries

The essence of boundaries and limits is knowing what we own and what we do not own. When we do not own ourselves as separate people from the ones we're bonded to, we develop unclear boundaries, and we allow people to cross those boundaries when we should be saying no.

Basic Boundaries

Your Body

Our most basic boundary is our body, and God wants us to possess our own body "in sanctification and honor" (1 Thess. 4:4 NASB). Whenever this boundary is crossed, we feel more like objects than people (pp. 146–48).

- Have your boundaries been crossed through physical or sexual abuse? Have rigid teachings kept you from enjoying the gift of marital sex?
- Did you learn growing up that admitting pain is wrong? Are you unable to feel and experience your body in meaningful ways?

- Have you crossed other people's boundaries through physical or sexual abuse? Have you apologized and asked for forgiveness?

Your Feelings

Your feelings, whether good or bad, are your property. They fall within your boundaries and are your responsibility. Other people's feelings are their responsibility. We should always be sensitive to the feelings of others, but we should never take responsibility for them. The Bible sends a clear message that we must be responsible to others, not for them (pp. 148–56).

- Do you feel responsible for other people's feelings? Describe a situation in which you have made a decision based on how others felt about your choices rather than on what you thought was right.
- Jesus cautions us against trying to make everyone happy (Luke 6:26) and warns that families are sometimes divided when someone follows his ways (Matt. 10:34–36). Are you reluctant to follow Christ in a certain direction because you know that your actions would leave other family members with negative feelings (anger, sadness, disappointment)? How?
- When has acknowledging your feelings helped you solve a problem or make a relationship better? When have you dealt with your anger either by confronting the one who sinned against you and forgiving that person or by giving up expectations from others that caused you to be angry? What happened when you did so?

Your Attitudes

Often we do not own our own attitudes; instead, we take responsibility for the attitudes of others and allow their expectations of us to shape what we do (pp. 156–59).

- Jesus calls us to remove the plank from our own eye so that we can "see clearly to remove the speck from [our] brother's eye" (Matt. 7:5). Whom are you blaming for problems that are caused by your own attitudes? What plank do you need to be dealing with?

- Who may be feeling victimized by your expectations? What "shoulds" do you have for other people?

- Whose expectations have made you feel victimized? From whom are you "feeling pressured" to do something? Can you figure out the process by which you got hooked into saying yes to something you are feeling pressured to do?

Your Behaviors

Being able to own our behavior is critical for having a sense of power and control over our lives. The law of sowing and reaping is the most trustworthy law of behavior (Prov. 4:26; Gal. 6:7–8), but it can be suspended when someone takes responsibility for another person's behavior and serves as a buffer for the consequences of his or her actions (pp. 159–62).

- When has someone not allowed you to suffer the consequences of your behavior? Why did that person do so? What did his or her actions accomplish? How did you end up suffering as a result? What lesson did you not learn because someone else shielded you from the consequences of what you had done? What lessons did you learn when you've had to deal with those consequences?

- When have you suffered the consequences for someone else's behavior and therefore not allowed him or her to "own" such behavior? Why did you do that? What did your actions accomplish?

Your Thoughts

As with feelings and attitudes, we must own our thoughts. After all, our thinking affects how we respond to people and situations. We must own all our critical thinking that discourages relationships, confess it, and allow God to change the way we think. At the same time, we cannot be responsible for the thoughts of others. If someone is thinking good or bad about us, we must accept it. We should listen to what people are saying and evaluate it; but if we are convinced in our heart that we are doing what is right, we must allow them the freedom to think whatever they want (see Luke 6:26) (pp. 162–64).

- When have your actions been influenced by the opinions, judgments, or condemnation of others rather than following what you knew to be right? Describe a situation in which that took place.
- What self-condemning thoughts haunt you (cf. Rom. 8:1)? What distortions, prejudices, and generalizations do you need to clear your property of?
- When have your opinions, judgments, or criticisms been ignored? How did you respond? Why? What boundaries were crossed in that situation?

Your Abilities

Crossed boundaries in the area of abilities come in two forms: trying to own what is someone else's property, and allowing someone else to own what is ours. We should never compare ourselves to others, for God made each of us unique (Rom. 12:6) (pp. 164–65).

- What does Galatians 6:4 mean to you?
- Do you tend to compare yourself to other people? Why are you so hard on yourself (false guilt)? Why do you think you are so in need of building yourself up (false pride)?
- Do you tend to compare, in their presence, your spouse, your children, your boss, or other important people in your life to someone else? Think of a specific occasion on which you did this; what damage did you do?
- When have you not been true to yourself with the ones you love most? What interests and abilities of yours have you denied in order to conform to their expectations? How do you feel about that?

Your Choices

The essence of boundaries is taking responsibility for ourselves, and the hub of responsibility is choice. God has given every human the ability to choose, so that we could choose to love him (Josh. 24:15). Boundaries are crossed whenever we make someone else's choices for them or whenever we think they are responsible for making our choices for us (pp. 165–70).

- When have others tried to bind you by making choices for you? What guilt messages have influenced you through the years? How have people tried to manipulate you? What specific methods did they use—threats, the silent treatment, "If-you-love-me-you-will . . ." statements, or name-calling?
- How have you made others responsible for your choices? When, for instance, have you agreed to do something you didn't really want to do and then griped about it? Why did you blame them instead of taking responsibility? What were you afraid of?
- How have you tried to bind others by making their choices for them? When have you said, "How could you do this to me?" and made other persons feel guilty for choices they made?

Your Desires

We must own our desires, and ours only. Our desires are our responsibility and not someone else's. We are to carry our own load and let other people carry theirs (Gal. 6:5). We will then see that owning our desires breeds responsibility and love (Matt. 7:12). Carrying someone else's desires will make us feel like victims (pp. 171–72).

- When have you blamed another person for your deprivation rather than seeing your desires as your responsibility and then working to fulfill them? When have you owned someone else's desire and, out of a sense of obligation rather than love, tried to fulfill it for them?
- When have you acknowledged someone else's desire as his/hers and acted out of love to fulfill that desire?
- When has someone blamed you for his or her deprivation rather than taking responsibility for that desire and working to fulfill it? When has someone owned

one of your desires and tried to fulfill it merely out of a sense of obligation? When has someone responded to one of your desires out of genuine love? How did you feel in each instance?

Your Limits

As we have seen with the other elements that lie within our boundaries, we must own our own limits. We must decide what limits we will set for ourselves and let others be responsible for their own limits. If we have limitations of time, money, or energy, we must set those. If we extend too far, it is our fault. At the same time, we cannot decide where someone else's limits are (pp. 172–76).

- Read Matthew 18:15–17 and 1 Corinthians 5:9–13. When have you had to draw the line against another person's evil behavior? How did that person respond to the limit you set?

- When has someone had to draw the line against your evil behavior? How did you respond? What effect did this incident have on your life?

- Where do you need to draw the line against a person's evil behavior? How can you tell if what you call patience, long-suffering, and forgiveness (good Christian virtues in and of themselves) are in fact enabling a person's evil behavior to continue?

- What are some of the limits you have had to draw so that you can live responsibly? Consider the areas we've been looking at—your body, feelings, attitudes, behaviors, thoughts, abilities, choices, and desires. Are your limits broad enough to enjoy God's blessings? Do you need more limits so that you can stop overextending yourself? See Exodus 18:17–18. Do you need to open the gates to your boundaries so that you can receive the good that God and others want to give you?

Our limits tell us much about where we end and someone else begins. With limits, we can know what we want versus what someone else wants and who is responsible for what.

- You've thought about times when your boundaries have been crossed. Who has crossed your boundaries most often in the past? How did they do that? What were the hurtful qualities of those relationships?

- What convictions and distortions did you develop in those relationships that need to be challenged and replaced with God's precepts? What philosophy of boundaries are you learning?

- Do you have a pattern of allowing others to cross your boundaries and limits? What is your pattern?

- When have you tried to make others feel responsible for things that you should have taken responsibility for? Whom did you hope would take responsibility?

- Is there a pattern of invading someone else's boundaries that you need to confess and turn from? To whom do you need to make restitution?

- What parts of your boundaries have you taken outside of time and when did that happen? For instance, when did you vow never to exercise your "no" muscle or your confrontational muscle?

When we own our body, feelings, attitudes, behaviors, thoughts, abilities, choices, and desires—and don't try to own other people's—we can figure out what we will allow in our lives and what we will not, so that evil will not take over. In addition, we can bring good in and out, as well as take out the bad through confession. Realizing our spiritual and emotional property line is the key to responsibility, freedom, and love.

- With whom do you have a good relationship at present—a relationship where boundaries are not crossed? What components of this relationship allow for mutual responsibility of all other aspects of ownership? How can you increase those elements? How can you respect others' boundaries more?

- To whom do you need to apply Matthew 18:15–17 and 1 Corinthians 5:9–13 right now? What is keeping you from doing so? What will be your first step?

- How have the boundary problems in your relationships reinforced your original beliefs about boundaries? How are these relationships injuring your sense of boundaries?

The essence of crossed boundaries is owning what is not ours and not owning what is ours. God has specific ways you can develop boundaries if you've never done so, and he will help you repair badly broken boundaries or build new ones. Rest assured that God can help you set boundaries and restore your damaged boundaries and your will.

- How can you change? How can God help?

God, you've opened my eyes to where I have crossed other people's boundaries, and I ask you to forgive me, and help me to ask them for forgiveness. You have also helped me see the various ways in which my boundaries—however weak or strong they were—have been crossed. Help me to extend to these people the kind of forgiveness I need to receive for crossing other people's boundaries. And enable me to take responsibility for the circumstances of my life that have resulted from having my boundaries crossed. As I continue to make changes that heal, help me to set wise and healthy boundaries. And, God, I ask you to restore those that have been damaged along the way. I pray in your Son's name. Amen.

LESSON 7

Learning to
Set Boundaries

Numerous problems arise when we fail to set and maintain good boundaries. If we do not realize what we are responsible for and what we are not responsible for, we can suffer from a variety of symptoms. You may recognize yourself in the following discussion of those symptoms (p. 177).

Symptoms of Failure to Set Boundaries

Symptoms point to the existence of an underlying problem. When people go for counseling, they usually talk about these symptoms, not about the underlying problem—the failure to set boundaries. The text gives a list of twenty-two symptoms that can point to a lack of boundaries (pp. 177–83).

- As you read the following list of symptoms, place a check mark next to any you have experienced. Then write down any words or phrases from the text that describe your experience and help you to better understand what is going on in your life.

- What has this list of symptoms shown you about yourself? Have you been trying to manage symptoms (codependency, identity confusion, substance abuse, generalized anxiety, etc.) rather than dealing with the root of the problem (failure to develop boundaries)?

Barriers to Creating Boundaries

With your review of the above list of symptoms, you may see more clearly than ever how you have failed to develop healthy boundaries for yourself. We must consider what has kept us from doing so. Past injury and distorted thinking can interfere with our attempts to create boundaries (p. 184).

Past Injury

To the degree that we have not been allowed in the past to own (take charge of) our bodies, feelings, attitudes, behaviors, thoughts, abilities, choices, wants, and limits, we are injured; and we will have boundary disturbances. In addition, we naturally resist taking responsibility for ourselves. Thus, when we suffer injury, taking responsibility is that much more difficult (p. 184).

- Who has not allowed you to own your own choices? Who has tried to make you feel responsible for their choices or the choices of others?
- At whose hand did you experience abuse, control, or guilt manipulation, three things that stunt the development of boundaries? What led you to allow it?

Distorted Thinking

As a result of injuries and our fallen condition, we distort God's reality. Straightening out what we are responsible for and what we are not responsible for is the key to establishing and maintaining boundaries (pp. 185–93).

- As you read the following list of distorted thoughts, place a check mark next to any that have taken up residence in your heart and mind.

- "I am bad for having boundaries."
- "I am selfish for owning my own life."
- "My wants are not important."
- "My wants are the only ones that are important."
- "I must have everything I want."
- "I am responsible for others."
- "I must do whatever anyone wants of me."
- "Whatever goes wrong is my fault."
- "Nothing is my fault."
- "They will hate me for saying no."
- "People will leave me for having my own boundaries."
- "People are controlling and want to manipulate me."
- "Others will resent my assertiveness and requests."
- "Others will leave me if I don't keep them happy."
- "Others are responsible for me."
- "People are selfish if they do not do what I want."
- "People are unloving if they say no to me."
- "People expect me to be compliant to their wishes."
- "Others are responsible for my behaviors."
- "God doesn't want me to own my life."
- "God doesn't want me to have anything of my own."
- "God wants me to have everything I want."
- "God thinks I'm selfish when I say no to others."
- "God wants me to allow others to do whatever they want to me or to others."
- "God doesn't want me to pursue what I want."
- "God is totally sovereign and in control; therefore I have no responsibility."
- "God is a 'hands-off' God and is not involved in my life."
- "If God says no to me, he doesn't love me."
- "God is forgiving and won't discipline me for my sin."
- "God is all limits and no love."

- What experiences have given you these distortions?
- What are you doing to counter these experiences and the resulting distortions?
- As you reviewed the distorted thoughts, where did you find hope?

Before looking at the specific skills needed to form and maintain boundaries, take a little more time to evaluate where your boundaries are today.

- What distortions of boundaries and limits are presently dominating you?
- When are you best at setting and realizing personal boundaries? Why?
- What are you doing to develop boundaries that you have let crumble or never had? What are you doing, for example, to develop your confrontational muscle that you once thought you could never exercise?
- To whom do you have difficulty saying no? Why?
- Whose "no" do you not respect and try to override?
- Whose boundaries are you overriding in other relationships? Why?
- What actions do you need to confess to God and others and receive forgiveness for? Whom do you need to confront in order to resolve some ongoing issue?

Learning to Set Boundaries

We have seen the importance of setting boundaries in our lives. We have looked at some who suffered because they did not learn how to set boundaries as they were growing up. Now let's look at some of the skills necessary for setting boundaries, for saying no when someone tries to cross those boundaries, and for maintaining the boundaries in your relationships with people who may or may not care to honor them (pp. 194–99).

- *Gain Awareness*—The questions in this workbook are designed to help you gain awareness of who you are—your body, feelings, attitudes, behaviors, thoughts, abilities, choices, wants, and limits. At this point, be sure to enlist the help of others to flesh out this picture of yourself. Let people who know you well help you get to know yourself (Prov. 15:22). Also, take a few minutes now to write down where you have come from, where you are now, and where you want to go.

- *Define Who You Are*—Begin to say what you feel, what you like, what you want, what you will do, and what you think. Make a pact with yourself to offer an opinion, to make a choice, to express a need, and to not say "I don't care" at least once when the opportunity arises this week—and have someone hold you accountable! Where will you begin this process?

- *Define Who You Are Not*—At the same time as you are defining who you are, say who you are not. In Proverbs 6:16–19, God takes a stand against certain things and announces his hatred of them; we must follow his example. So decide to say what you don't agree with, don't like, and won't do this week instead of remaining quiet and merely fitting in with the crowd. Again, have your safe friend hold you accountable!

- *Develop Your "No" Muscle*—God says no to certain things (see Exod. 20:1–17), and we must do the same. Plan to say no sometime this week—and start small. In what relatively minor situation will you test your "no" muscle? Realize that when you do so, you don't need to make any excuses or take responsibility for the other person's disappointment.

- *Stop Blaming Others*—We reap what we sow (Gal. 6:7), and in this fallen world we often reap what others sow. Not blaming them for the circumstances of your life does not mean that they did not cause your trouble; it simply means that you will deal with that trouble. What trouble will you start dealing with today? What will be your first step? Are you willing to accept the responsibility for dealing with the effects of injury that was not your fault?

- *Stop Playing Victim*—As an adult, you make choices, and you are responsible for what you choose to do. In what situation are you feeling like a victim? What choices have you made that have put you in that situation? What new feelings come with the perspective on the situation as presented in this chapter?

- *Persevere*—God commands us to persevere (Heb. 12:1–3), and perseverance develops discipline, responsibility, character, and hope (Rom. 5:3–4). We practice perseverance as we work toward our goals. Note and examine when you "bail out" on persevering. Why? Who can help?

- *Become Active, Not Reactive*—People with boundary problems often make choices by passively reacting to others. Look at ways to live out your values in conflict situations instead of reacting in defensive ways. Where and with whom do you need to be firm and loving?

- *Set Limits*—If you are suffering from another person's abusive behavior, wait no longer to put limits on what you will tolerate (Matt. 18:15–17; 1 Cor. 5:9–13). Plan what you will say, deliver that message, and then follow through on what you say you will do if that person doesn't change his or her behavior. For whom will you set limits? Who will support you?

- Also, begin to recognize your limits of time, money, and energy. Where are you sowing sparingly (2 Cor. 9:6)? Where are you sowing more than you have to give? Ask God to show you and get input from other people to find out what is reasonable for you at this time.

- *Choose Values*—The Bible teaches what God values (see, for example, 1 Sam. 15:22; Matt. 5:3–11; Luke 16:13; 1 Cor. 13; Gal. 5:22–23). What values have you been living by? What values do you want to be living by? Are you shaping your values by God's values? What will you do to start living by values you can own?

- What direction have you been heading in your life without really owning it? What direction do you want your life to be taking? What steps will you take to begin going in the direction you want to be going?

- *Practice Self-Control*—A person who lacks self-control is "like a city whose walls are broken through" (Prov. 25:28). Do you need to exercise self-control and limit your wishes, your feelings? Are your limits on your wishes and your feelings perhaps too narrow? Enlist a trusted friend to help you determine how to strike a balance between satisfying your desires and controlling them.

- *Accept Others*—If you want to feel accepted, accept others. If you want others to respect your no, respect their no. Only when you love people when they say no and grant them their freedom will you yourself be free—and we are to love and accept one another because God first loved us (1 John 4:19). Whom do you need to learn to love and accept for who they are? Whose no do you need to respect?

- *Realize Your Separateness*—God made you (Ps. 139:13–16; 1 Cor. 12), and he delights in those characteristics which make you unique. List ways you are different from your loved ones, as well as ways you are like them.

- How much time do you spend by yourself? Realize that separateness and time apart enhance a relationship. What change in your schedule can you make to find a little more time for yourself? What interest will you choose that is yours alone? Plan what you will do to develop it, and then take the first step.

- *Be Honest*—The Lord calls us to be truthful (Prov. 12:22). Truth and honesty bring people closer together in their relationships. With whom and about what do you tend to be less than honest in your relationships? Why do you hesitate to tell loved ones what you really think? When during the coming week will you risk telling someone who is safe what you really think?

- *Challenge Distorted Thinking*—Jesus taught that the truth sets us free (John 8:32). Look again at the list of distorted thoughts earlier in this lesson and review which ones have taken up residence in your heart and mind. Now, with the help of God's Spirit, determine what the truth really is and ask him to help you to live according to that truth. What is the first step you will take? As with every change you make, enlist the help of friends as you practice these new ways of being.

Responsibility

In looking at boundaries, we cannot escape one main point: responsibility. Our boundaries basically define for us our areas of responsibility. They tell us what our lives consist of and what we are responsible for. We must own our own bodies, feelings, attitudes, behaviors, thoughts, abilities, choices, desires, and limits (pp. 198–99).

- As you evaluate the future in terms of the problems you see in your boundaries and the way you have been dealing with other people's boundaries, what are you going to change? How?
- Knowing that it takes relationship and truth to change, whose help are you going to get for your plan?
- Think about people whose boundaries you have crossed. Which situations will you confront now? What will you do and when? How will you apologize?
- Think, too, about the people who have crossed your boundaries. Which situations will you confront now? What will you do—and when? What do you expect these people to do when you confront them? How will you deal with their reactions?
- In what specific ways are you going to challenge your distorted thinking and overcome the barriers to setting boundaries?
- What difficulties do you envision as you begin to create boundaries for yourself? How will you negotiate those difficulties?
- Whom will you get to listen to you, pray for you, and support you as you live out your plan?

Again, we must own our bodies, feelings, attitudes, behaviors, thoughts, abilities, choices, desires, and limits. Only then can we choose to give ourselves away in love just as Christ did. Owning our own lives is the essence of freedom, and there is no love without freedom. When you give before you are free and truly own yourself, you fall short of servanthood and into slavery. When you realize what you own and then share yourself with others, you fulfill the law of Christ.

God, thank you for continuing to open my eyes and helping me better understand the things I do, the thoughts I think, the hurts I've felt, and the relationships in which I struggle. Please bring healing where past injuries make it difficult for me to establish healthy boundaries. And let the light of your truth clarify and correct my distorted thinking about myself, about other people, and about you.

I ask, too, Lord, that you would give me the wisdom and courage needed as I develop skills to set boundaries. May your Spirit help me live out these powerful truths that I'm learning about—the freedom and responsibility that come with establishing and maintaining healthy boundaries. May your Spirit enable me to fulfill your law by first showing me who I am and then enabling me to give myself away. I pray in the name of Jesus. Amen.

PART 3

Sorting Out
Good
–and–
Bad

LESSON 8

What Is the Problem?

We are both good and bad. The people around us are good and bad. Our natural tendency, however, is to try to resolve this problem by keeping the good and the bad separated. This creates a split in our experience of ourselves, others, and the world around us—a split that is not based on reality and cannot stand the test of time and real life (p. 204).

The Problem of Splitting Good and Bad

Trying to keep the good and the bad separated results in an inability to tolerate badness, weakness, and failure in ourselves and others (p. 204).

- Evaluate your ability to tolerate badness, weakness, and failure in yourself. What about yourself do you find hardest to accept?
- How well do you tolerate other people's badness, weakness, and failure? When are you most condemning?

Splitting good and bad leads to two basic problems. Sometimes we deny the existence of bad, while at other times, we deny the existence of good. If we do not have the ability to tolerate and deal with the simultaneous existence of good and bad, we cannot successfully deal with and live in this world, for the world and we are precisely that: good and bad (pp. 204–5).

- Describe a time when you felt thoroughly bad because you failed at something.
- Do you tend to feel thoroughly good when life is going well?
- When have you blamed or punished someone for failing to be the all-good person you wanted him or her to be? Who was that person?
- Have you denied another person's real badness and continued on in an unhealthy relationship? If so, when?
- What have you devalued (a church, a group, a job) because it hasn't met your standards of perfection? Explain.

A Biblical Perspective of Good and Bad

The world was not always both good and bad. In the beginning, everything was "all good." The creation was without blemish (Gen. 1–2). Human beings were without sin (p. 205).

- List three or four times when you have gotten a glimpse of the perfection God intended for his creation, for us his people, and for our relationships with him and with each other.

God created us for perfection, but now we find ourselves living somewhere else — and we are not prepared to live in an imperfect world. We were not made to deal with the effects of the fall. Our spirits are much too tender to live in a world of hurtful people. We do not have enough grace inside to anesthetize us against the pain of our own badness. Furthermore, we feel utter fear and terror of God instead of overwhelming awe and love (pp. 205–6).

- When have you rejected a friend, a spouse, a child, a church, a job, or a hobby as soon as badness appeared?

- When have you pronounced something totally bad the minute one aspect of it was not perfect? Explain.
- When have you been rejected as soon as some of your badness appeared?

If we are to negotiate life well, we must find a way to live in a world that has both good and bad, a world where, Jesus promises, we "will have trouble" (John 16:33).

The Ideal Self

We all have a distant memory of what we were meant to be. We can all imagine what a perfect "me" would be like. The Bible itself sets forth some traits of the ideal woman and the ideal man (Prov. 31; Eph. 4:14–15; 1 Tim. 3; Titus 1:6–9) and speaks of a time when the lost ideal will be recovered (Rom. 8:22–25) (pp. 206–8).

- Think for a second about the perfect you. Describe some of the traits you would have.
- Think, too, about the possibility of doing perfectly everything you can do. Share some details of this fantasy.

The Real Self

Deep down inside, we all realize the difference between our ideal self, the perfect self we would like to be, and our real self, the one that truly is. If these two battle each other, we will be in constant conflict. The real self is, in Paul's words, "unspiritual, sold as a slave to sin" (Rom. 7:14) (pp. 208–9).

- Identify some of your areas of weakness. Where do you fail? Where do you sin?
- Where are you broken? Where have you been injured? Where are you immature and emotionally underdeveloped?

The Relationship between the Ideal and the Real

If our ideal self is at war with our real self, the ideal will judge the real whenever it appears, bring down condemnation on it, and try to make it hide. And when we are hiding, we are not in relationship with God and others. This is the inherent problem in the relationship between the ideal and the real. When the ideal and the real self find themselves adversaries, they naturally move further and further apart (pp. 209–10).

- Richard did not accept his anger or his childlikeness; his ideal self had decided that they should not be a part of him. What parts of you do you not accept?
- Are you demanding perfection of yourself? What actions and emotions betray your belief that you should be ideal and that no imperfection should live in you?
- What real but less-than-ideal parts of other people do you tend not to accept? Whom do you struggle to accept? Is there a pattern?

An important aspect of the relationship between the ideal and the real is its emotional tone. If we adopt a judgmental tone, our ideals will condemn our real self into nonexistence. If we adopt a loving and accepting tone toward our real self, there is hope for transformation. If we, like the apostle Paul (Rom. 7:15–19; 8:1), are able to accept the parts of ourselves we do not feel are ideal, then those parts will be loved and healed. And it goes without saying that we should never condemn ourselves for those elements in our nature that belong to our natural humanness; God does not expect us to be superhuman (pp. 211–13).

- What has been the emotional tone of the relationship between your ideal and your real self? Has your ideal self been judgmental or accepting of your real self?
- Why do you think your ideal self responds to your real self as it does? Whose attitudes from the past are you reflecting?
- When have your demands that you be perfect made you miserable or ruined a relationship? When have you suffered from completely letting go of standards and ideals?
- When have your demands that another person be perfect made that person miserable or ruined a relationship?
- When has another person's demands that you be perfect made you miserable or ruined a relationship?

In a life where the real self is loved and accepted, it can be encouraged to grow toward the ideal. In a life where standards are accepted and cherished as goals and our true self is accepted and loved, there will be peace and growth. This view of ourselves is consistent with the Bible's teaching that we are created in the image of God, that we have incredible value, and that we are sinful and broken (Gen. 1:27; Ps. 8:5–8; Rom. 3:10). Both this ideal and this reality are present in the Bible, and both need to be reconciled into a grace-giving relationship with God and others (pp. 212–13).

Distortions of the Ideal

Some people have a distorted idea of what a human being can be. What some think is ideal was never really part of the way God created us. What others think we can regain (perfection) was lost in the fall. Either way, these ideal selves are not real. We must confront the demands of our ideal self and accept what is true (pp. 213–15).

- How have you distorted your ideal self? Would your ideal not need other people, be without sexual feelings, not get angry or sad, never work, or be something else that runs counter to what God created human beings to be?
- Another distortion of the ideal self comes when people feel bad about things that should be acknowledged as good but were not accepted as such in their family (such as showing emotions and setting boundaries). What good things were not accepted in the family you grew up in and have resulted in a distortion of the ideal?

Our ideal self is a system of internalized values growing out of our upbringing as well as our own wishes for ourselves. The important point is that whatever is true, but is not acceptable to the ideal, gets judged and dismissed in some way or another.

Dealing with the Good and Bad Conflict

We deal with the conflict between the good and the bad in our lives in four different ways, three of which always fail. We need to examine ourselves, how we have dealt with the conflict between the good and the bad (pp. 215–19).

- *Denial of the Bad*—We are not to deny our badness, for that is the sin of pride (Matt. 23:25–27). Nor are we to deny the badness of others: we are all equal sinners (Rom. 3:23). Which of the following have you denied in yourself because they are not a part of your ideal self: negative emotions (such as anger, fear, sadness, grief, pain) and sinful feelings (such as lust, envy, pride, bitterness)? Do you try to make sure other people do not see or address the bad in you? For whom have you tried to appear perfect?

- Have you denied the bad in other people? Whom have you idealized? What has resulted from these denials?

- *Denial of the Good*—When some people feel overwhelmed by the demands of the ideal that they, as sinners, cannot fulfill, they do away with standards and deny the good altogether (Rom. 1:18–23). Have you denied the good standard of God?

- Have you denied the good in other people? In whom? Have you denied the existence of absolute good? What has resulted from these denials?

- Describe an instance when someone has denied the good in you. Who was it? What did that feel like?

- *Attack and Judge*—Attacking and judging is the most common way of dealing with the bad, but such an attack on the real self is condemning and hurtful. The Bible calls it "worldly sorrow" and teaches that it "brings death" (2 Cor. 7:10). Do you angrily attack your real self with harsh words of judgment? Do you see both good and bad in other people but attack their badness?

- *Acceptance*—Clearly, denying the good, denying the bad, and attacking and judging are ineffective ways of sorting out good and bad. The fourth alternative—the biblical alternative and the only one that works—is acceptance. It is called grace and truth. When we accept our real self, we grasp onto both the good and the bad at the same time. We are not angry and condemning. We accept and forgive the bad, while clinging to the ideal as an unrealized goal. And we need to do this for others as well as for ourselves (Rom. 15:7; Eph. 4:32; Col. 3:12–13) (pp. 218–19).

- What part of your real self are you becoming more accepting of? Why are you struggling to accept yourself?

- As you consider important relationships, whose real self do you need to be more accepting of? What resistance are you finding in your heart as you think about accepting them? How will you demonstrate your acceptance of these people?
- What does Proverbs 17:9 tell you about the value of accepting others and being kind to them?

A Developmental Perspective

If not resolving issues of good and bad is so destructive, then why don't we just do it? Why don't we just accept the bad and value the good? The answer lies in the nature of the fall. We were never intended to handle the coexistence of good and bad. But we sinned and found ourselves in a tough spot: Having been born without knowledge of grace, we need to internalize grace in order to learn how to accept the bad without rejecting relationship. It is in relationship that we begin to internalize love and forgiveness or their opposites, and our relationship to our parents is the first source of these lessons for life (pp. 219–22).

- What did your parents teach you about forgiveness? Failure? Anger? Pain? Fear? How to deal with the bad in you?
- When you were growing up, was there enough good and forgiveness for you to tolerate the bad in yourself and other people? Was there enough forgiveness for you to learn to forgive yourself and other people?
- When you were growing up, did your parents frustrate you enough that you learned to accept less than ideal in other people? Or have you idealized your doting or "ideal" parents, who are not as perfect as you may think?
- If you are a parent, what are you teaching your children about forgiveness? Failure? Anger? Fear? How to deal with their bad sides? Is there enough good and forgiveness for your children to be able to tolerate the bad in themselves and other people? Is there enough frustration that your children are learning to forgive themselves and other people?

When we are not able to tolerate good and bad together, we see people as good only if they are gratifying and bad if they are not. We are not able to forgive the "good guy" who makes mistakes. But when our frailties are understood and loved by others, we learn to accept them into our picture of ourselves and to value our real selves. And we also learn to forgive and accept the real self of others with their limitations. The scriptural principle is that we love and forgive because we have been loved and forgiven (Luke 7:36–47) (pp. 219–22).

Love and Acceptance

Love is the solution and resolution to all problems of good and bad. If we have enough love with limits, or grace with truth, we begin to experience the way God relates to us and to learn that we are standing in grace (Rom. 5:2), where judgment and condemnation do not come into the picture. We experience badness and failure as a sad thing, for it causes us to miss out on loving someone (p. 222).

- Think for a moment about the persistent sins you struggle with. How are you missing out on real love by sinning?
- How does your sin hurt you? Why is this perspective on your sin more helpful to your efforts to be free of it than calling yourself a bad person or condemning and being angry with yourself?

When we see our failures and sin as a lack of love for another person instead of "badness," then we have moved to a more mature way of seeing issues of good and bad. Furthermore, it is only when we are no longer condemned for the bad that we can let go of it and walk after the Spirit. Sin loses its power, for grace has set us free (Rom. 7:24; 8:1) (p. 223).

- When have you received "no condemnation" from someone when you confessed your sin? From whom did you receive it? How did you respond to that grace, an extension of God's grace?

- Maybe you've never received the feeling of "no condemnation" because you've never risked confessing your sins to another person. Who might be safe? Will you now go to that person and let him or her extend God's grace to you?
- To whom in your life do you need to extend God's grace and offer "no condemnation" for their sin, confessed or not?

Accept the Sinner, Hate the Sin

We are sinners who have been forgiven. In Paul's words, we are accepted "in the One he loves" (Eph. 1:6). The real issue we face is the sin, not the sinner. We should be heartbroken before God because of our sins, but we should never condemn ourselves as persons, for Christ took on himself our condemnation. "There is now no condemnation for those who are in Christ Jesus" (Rom. 8:1) (pp. 224–25).

- Are you on a merry-go-round of feeling that you are good when you do good things, and then feeling you are bad when you sin?
- Write out the truth of Hebrews 10:14, 17 and insert your name where appropriate.
- The issue of guilty versus not guilty, or good versus bad, has been dealt with in Jesus "once for all" (Heb. 7:27). He has made us acceptable. Therefore the question is not, "Are we good or bad?" but "What are we doing?" When has pondering the question, "Am I good or bad?" led you to focus on your guilt or on how you compare to other people rather than on God's grace and the ability to change, which he gives?
- The question "What am I doing?" has as its corollary, "Am I hurting God, myself, or someone else by this behavior?" What can the grief that comes with answering this question move you to do?

Grief over hurt that we are inflicting, called "godly sorrow," will move us not to punish ourselves or anyone else but to take care of the one being hurt. This is the essence of a love-based morality, and this "no condemnation" transforms lives. When we do not feel condemned nor fear condemnation no matter what we do, we are well on the way to being more loving, for those who are forgiven much, love much (see Luke 7:44–47). This is the nature of the relationship between the ideal and the real—one of correction toward a goal of love instead of one of anger and attack toward the real self who fails (p. 225).

- Whom are you hurting right now with certain behaviors and attitudes? From whom can you receive "no condemnation" and the total acceptance that will help free you from those behaviors and attitudes?
- Again, to whom do you need to offer "no condemnation" and the total acceptance that will help free that person from the behaviors and attitudes that are hurting you and him or her?

As we seek forgiveness and seek to be forgiving, we do well to remember that God says we are incredibly wonderful, extremely sinful, beset with all sorts of weakness, and overflowing with talents (Pss. 8:4–6; 103:14; Rom. 3:10). Try to think of all of that at one time. It's a real exercise in the task of resolving good and bad, a task we will continue in the next two lessons.

God, how gracious is your view of us. And how far it is from my view of myself and my view of other people. I realize how much I have to learn about the presence of good and bad in the world, in people, and in myself. I also see that I have a lot to unlearn from my childhood and youth. Replace my distorted ideas about good and bad with your truth of grace and love.

As you do so, God, I ask that you enable my ideal self to be less judgmental and more accepting of my real self. Teach me to be less judgmental and more accepting of other people as well. Help me to accept and resolve my feelings that aren't sinful but are negative and seem bad—my feelings of anger, sadness, fear, and grief. Free me, too, from my tendency to deny the bad, deny the good, and attack and judge—both myself and other people—rather than to accept the good and the bad at the same time.

God, I thank you that you value me with all my frailties and sin and that you accept me in my limitations with an unconditional love that frees me rather than condemns me. May I internalize your "no condemnation," believe it for myself, and offer it to others. And as I experience your "no condemnation," help me to grieve over the hurt I've inflicted, let go of my sin, and become more loving. I pray in the name of your Son, my Savior. Amen.

LESSON 9

When We Fail to Accept Good and Bad

Failing to Accept Good and Bad

Like it or not, we live in an imperfect world. As we all know, the world is not purely "good." Fortunately, however, the world is not purely "bad" either. Rather, the world, the people around us, and we ourselves are a mixture of good and bad. People who can't deal with this fact often develop a variety of problems in their day-to-day life (pp. 226–29).

- Review the discussion of the problems that can arise if we don't accept the mixture of good and bad in the world and society. On the list below, place a check mark next to any problems you've encountered. Then write down any words or phrases from the text that describe your experience and help you better understand what is going on in your life.
- What has this list of problems shown you about yourself? Have you been trying to manage symptoms (such as perfectionism, an inability to tolerate weakness, self-image problems, anxiety, guilt) rather than dealing with the root of the

problem—the failure to accept good and bad? How has this failure affected your relationships?

Barriers to Resolving Good and Bad

Having reviewed the list of problems above, you may see more clearly than ever how you have failed to accept the coexistence of good and bad in the world, in people, and in yourself. Why? Past injury and distorted thinking often interfere with our attempts to resolve good and bad (pp. 230–35).

Past Injury

Having been born without knowledge of grace, we need to internalize grace in order to learn how to accept the bad without rejecting the relationship. But often that internalization of grace doesn't happen, and often our life experiences reinforce the split between good and bad.

- Who denied your badness in the past and destructively saw you as without fault or weakness? Why did you allow this?

- Who denied your good parts and saw you as all bad? How did you respond?

- Whose badness in the past have you denied? Do you see it now? Have you faced how bad they actually were, or do you tend to take responsibility for their badness or weaknesses?

- Whose goodness did you deny and whom did you see as all bad? Do you still see that person that way?

- When and to whom have you tried to appear all good or ideal? How did this affect your relationship? What would you do differently now?

- To whom in the past did you feel safe to confess your badness or weakness to? What qualities in this person made you feel safe to be less than ideal?

- When did you try to hide your weakness from those who accepted you? Why? How has this affected your relationship?

- When did you not take into account your own good? What were the results?
- We are to forgive one another as God has forgiven us in Christ (Eph. 4:32). Is there anyone anywhere whom you have not forgiven? How is this hurting you?
- God calls us to confess our sins to him and to one another (James 5:16; 1 John 1:9). What do you need forgiveness for? What is keeping you from bringing this into the light by admitting it to God and to a safe friend who loves you?

Distorted Thinking

Our inability to resolve issues of good and bad result in distorted thinking about ourselves, others, and God. The book lists twenty-one possible ideas of such thinking that can take up residence in our hearts and minds (pp. 230–35).

- Place a check mark next to any of the following ideas that have taken up residence in your heart and mind.
  - "I am really not worth loving."
  - "My badness is worse than anyone else's."
  - "I have unacceptable feelings."
  - "I should be better than I am."
  - "I am ideal."
  - "I am unforgivable."
  - "I can't stand an imperfect world."
  - "I have no strengths or talents."
  - "People will dislike me for my badness."
  - "They will attack me for my weakness."
  - "They don't have feelings like this."
  - "They will leave me if they find out that . . ."
  - "They will not like me if I am not all bad."
  - "They will respect my Christian walk only if I am perfect."
  - "God expects me to be all good."

- ⊙ "God accepts me when I am good and rejects me when I am bad. Then he will accept me again when I am good."
- ⊙ "God is shocked at times by me."
- ⊙ "God will reject me if I do . . ."
- ⊙ "God is keeping track of my badness."
- ⊙ "God thinks immaturity is bad."
- ⊙ "God cannot understand my struggle."
- What experiences gave you these distortions?
- What are you doing to counter these experiences and the resulting distortions?
- As you review the discussion in the book of these distorted thoughts, where do you find hope in their refutations?

The distortions listed above form the prison that houses the real self. Satan has always tried to trick us into believing lies, and he steals lives through the lies and distortions. We need to confront the lies, see where they come from, and rebuke them in the mighty name of Jesus (p. 235).

Accepting Good and Bad

In the next chapter, we will learn more about how to accept good and bad together. Before doing so, however, take a prayerful inventory of the present and see if you are avoiding issues of good and bad.

With whom do you have a safe confessional process now? Do you feel free to show them (him, her) your badness and weakness? Do you show all of it? What enables you to do so in this relationship?

- Who denies your badness at present and makes you all good? How is this destructive? Why are you allowing it?
- Who denies your good parts at present and makes you all bad? Why do you allow it?

- Whom are you seeing as all good? Why?
- Whom are you seeing as all bad? Why?
- To whom have you been angry and condemning? Why?
- Whom are you not forgiving? Why?
- How and where are you hiding weakness and badness? Why? How is it hurting you?
- Where are you expending energy to appear ideal to others? Why?

Distorted thinking about goodness and badness is learned in the context of relationships. We internalize how we are treated in those relationships. If we are to be free of that distortion and free to live in God's truth, we must put ourselves into situations where we can learn God's ways of relating to us. That's part of what we'll look at in the next lesson.

God, I now see quite clearly how my inability to separate good and bad and accept them as existing together in your world, in people, and in myself has affected my life. By your Spirit, show me how I can be free from the problems that have come with my failure to accept good and bad. I also see how distorted some of my thinking is. Again, I ask that the light of your truth will clarify and correct my distorted thinking about myself, about other people, and about you.

And, Lord, I am understanding how much I need to rest in your grace, your forgiveness, and your love. Thank you that you accept the bad as well as the good in me. In relationships with your people, may I come to know that kind of acceptance experientially and not just intellectually. Give me the courage to enter into such relationships of grace that I may accept my real self and the real self of the people around me more graciously. I pray in Jesus' name. Amen.

LESSON 10

Learning to Accept
Both Good and Bad

The First Step

The place where we all need to live in relation to the issue of good and bad is one of "no condemnation." But how do we get there emotionally? The first step is to look at the emotional nature of our relationship between the ideal and the real (p. 236).

- Is the internal relationship between your ideal self and your real self a relationship of loving acceptance and correction toward a loving goal? Do you see your failures as something to learn from?
- Or do you split good and bad? Do you condemn and punish yourself and others for failures? Are you angry toward your real self and the bad that is there? Do you see your failures as something to hide?
- How did you learn your loving acceptance or your angry condemnation? How well does your approach, whichever one it is, serve you today?

Why We Split Good and Bad

Angry condemnation does not serve us well. To change that approach, we must look first at where that split between good and bad came from. A wrong relationship between the real and the ideal comes from two sources: nature and nurture. Regarding nature, we are born with a "wish to be like God," and we are born under the law with a fallen conscience that punishes us for failing in any way (pp. 236–37).

- What do the following Scriptures teach about our human nature?
  - Genesis 3:6–7, 10
  - Isaiah 14:13–14
  - James 2:10

Furthermore, we are nurtured by imperfect people who relate to us imperfectly. They often act toward us in anger when we fail, reinforcing our condemning conscience (p. 237).

- What parts of your parents' critical natures have you internalized? What harsh, judgmental words that they used are part of your thinking about yourself? Where is your own critical nature most active?
- What parts of your parents' loving and accepting natures have you internalized? What words of unconditional acceptance that they used are part of your thinking about yourself?

How We Get Good and Bad Back Together

However severe the split between good and bad is in your mind, you must know that you can get good and bad back together. Forgiving relationships within the church—relationships of grace—can cure the problem of splitting good and bad and move us out of our unloved state. One of our tasks as members of the body of Christ is to accept and love each other in spite of our failures and to gently correct each other toward a goal of love. We'll look at three important medicines for curing the split between good and bad (pp. 237–44).

Confession

James writes, "Confess your sins to each other and pray for each other so that you may be healed" (James 5:16). Christians know they must confess their sins to God, but this is only half the issue. They must also confess their sins to each other (p. 237).

- To whom have you felt safe to confess your badness or weakness—your sin? What qualities in that person made you feel safe to be less than ideal? What did he or she do to make you feel loved and forgiven after you had confessed your sin? How did that person's acceptance of you help you feel God's forgiveness?
- What has kept you in the past from confessing your sins to another person? What is keeping you from doing so now?

Paul instructs us to "accept one another, then, just as Christ accepted you" (Rom. 15:7). If, when we confess our offenses to one another, we are accepted in spite of them, we begin to internalize that acceptance and become more loving toward our real self (p. 237).

- When and how have you seen Jesus transform your badness, once you brought it into the light? When and how have you seen Jesus work in another person's life, when that individual confessed his or her sins?

When we hide our badness, it gets worse. Furthermore, we are keeping these attitudes and behaviors separated from grace, truth, and time; and they are then not able to grow and change. When we confess this buried part to God, he will begin to cleanse and heal it (Ps. 51:7; 1 John 1:7, 9). When we confess it to others, they can begin to accept us and heal our isolation. We move into a loved position (pp. 238–39).

- What attitudes and behaviors—what soul-killers—do you need to confess to God and to other people? What buried parts of yourself do you need to lay before God for cleansing and healing and before others for their loving acceptance?
- If you have never confessed your sin to another person, who is safe for you to begin to do so now? Who will love you and offer you the grace of God? Write down when you plan to get together with that person.

Confess your dark wounded places to someone who will incarnate God's love and acceptance. Doing so will allow the light of Christ to touch those places and nullify the laws that force "unacceptable" aspects into hiding.

Forgiveness

A second important ingredient in curing the good-bad split is forgiving others. Jesus said, "If you do not forgive others their sins, your Father will not forgive your sins" (Matt. 6:15), and he calls us to have mercy on one another just as God has had mercy on us (Matt. 18:33–35). Paul echoes this teaching: "Be kind and compassionate to one another, forgiving each other, just as in Christ God forgave you" (Eph. 4:32) (p. 240).

- Do you struggle with forgiving others? Do you struggle with accepting that God has completely forgiven you, and do you continue to try to earn his acceptance? Often these two struggles are related.
- Do you struggle to forgive those who have hurt you because you still want repayment from them? How is this attitude affecting you emotionally and spiritually?
- When have you finally forgiven someone for something? What did you experience as a result?
- From whom have you been withholding forgiveness? When will you free yourself from that bondage to him or her and extend forgiveness?

Choosing not to forgive is choosing bitterness. It is choosing to be connected to the person who wronged you. When we can sever that tie through forgiveness and accept those who have hurt us just as God has accepted us, then we are free to integrate our own "bad" and unforgiven parts (p. 240).

The Integration of Negative Emotions

Many people conceal their negative feelings of anger, sadness, and fear, resulting in depression, anxiety, and fear of relationships. Negative feelings, however, are valid, and they must be dealt with so that they won't cause problems (pp. 240–41).

Anger—Anger is good because it tells us that something is wrong and signals that we are in danger of losing something that matters to us. We need to respond to the danger, but we must not sin as we attempt to resolve the problem (Eph. 4:26) (pp. 241–42).

- Give a specific example when anger told you that something was wrong or alerted you to the danger of losing something that mattered to you.
- When have you responded to anger and been able to protect yourself or someone you care about from danger?
- When have you held on to or denied your anger and have it become bitterness and a foothold for Satan?
- Do you need to get more in touch with some long-held anger that you've been holding off? How will you determine its source? What is your anger cueing you to try to protect? What will you do to own it? What will you do to process it?

Sadness—Sadness signals hurt and loss. It helps us grieve and let go. It is always the path to joy because it signals a hurt that needs to be processed. Another aspect of sadness is tenderness. As one major aspect of the image of God, our sadness must be protected at all costs. If we can't feel sad, we get coldhearted (pp. 242–43).

- Describe an experience when you walked the path of sadness and ended up in a place of joy.

- How has feeling sadness kept your heart tender and sensitive? When have you found your heart hardened by not letting yourself feel sadness? Where are you now on this continuum between a tender and a hardened heart?
- When have you been unable to feel the sadness that circumstances called for? What kept you from doing so? What is keeping you from doing so now?
- What current circumstances in your life—what hurts and losses—are prompting feelings of sadness? What are you doing with those feelings?

Fear—Fear is another emotion that signals danger. The danger may be real or imaginary, but we must be aware of it if we are to work through it. Denying fear keeps us out of touch with our humble position in the universe and keeps us away from God. It is our fear and lack of control over much of life that leads us to our heavenly Father. We must be in touch with our fears to get to a position of need—our need for other people as well as for God (pp. 243–44).

- What fears have helped you protect yourself? What fears have immobilized you?
- When have you, aware of your fears, chosen to trust God? Would you have turned to God at the time if you hadn't acknowledged your fear?
- What fears do you need to acknowledge now? What dangers are they alerting you to? What will you do with your fears? How will you bring God into the picture?

Other Skills Needed to Integrate Good and Bad

Growth does not come without effort. We must learn and practice many skills in order to resolve issues of the good and the bad. Here are some (pp. 244–46).

- *Prayer*—Besides confessing your sins, ask God to make you aware of things you may be ignoring. Take a few minutes now to pray David's prayer: "Search me, God, and know my heart; test me and know my anxious thoughts. See if there is any offensive way in me, and lead me in the way everlasting" (Ps. 139:23–24). What did God reveal to you? Did you remember to ask for forgiveness?

- *Rework the Ideal*—What needs to be eliminated from your picture of what an ideal you would be? Don't hesitate to delete those ideas that come from your family or the culture instead of from God (Prov. 31; Eph. 4:14–15).

- *Rework Distortions*—The Scriptures say much about our ideal, our reality, God, and salvation. What is the first topic you will study and when will you begin?

- *Monitor the Relationship between the Ideal and the Real*—Make an effort to listen to the way you respond to the less than ideal. Do you deny it? Do you deny the good? Do you attack and judge? Do you accept and forgive? Note especially where you need to replace your harsh words of judgment with words of grace and acceptance.

- *Practice Loving the Less Than Ideal in Others*—No human being is righteous (Rom. 3:10). We fail, we sin, we are bad as well as good, and we need to accept that less than ideal in others as well as in ourselves. So plan to stay connected the next time someone you are in relationship with is less than ideal. Whom do you tend to disregard when "badness" appears? How will you handle the situation next time?

- *Do Not Discard Others When They Are Less Than Perfect*—Christ died for us sinners; he didn't wait for us to be perfect to offer his love (Rom. 5:8). We must follow his example. Do you find yourself going from friend to friend, spouse to spouse, church to church? What are you going to do to correct this pattern?

- *Process and Value Negative Feelings*—Negative feelings are not as bad as you fear they are, so don't avoid them. Prepare yourself mentally and emotionally to feel and deal with anger, sadness, pain, and fear the next time the opportunity arises. Remember, too, that the goal is not only awareness of these feelings but also acknowledgment of them. With whom will you share these feelings?

- *Expect Badness and Weakness from Everyone*—Be realistic: Everyone—including you—has good and bad, strengths and weaknesses (Rom. 3:10). How will you readjust your expectations? Will you embrace others and love them when their faults surface?

- *Expect Faults from the Creation*—Expect things to go wrong (Rom. 8:22) and don't be surprised when they do. How will you adjust your standards so that you can relax and accept good and bad as it comes?

Some Action Steps

Now that you have considered some of the skills needed to integrate the good and the bad, plan to take some specific action steps to do so in your life.

- Whose badness do you need to confront? When and how will you do that?
- Whose goodness do you need to appreciate? How will you let them know?
- With whom can you begin to share your real self? Why are they a good choice to let in on those parts of you?
- What will you do to take your good parts out of hiding?
- What aspects of your ideal self will you begin to get in line with a true ideal as God sees it?
- How will you work on your relationship between the ideal and the real? How will you make it more forgiving?
- What imperfections in others and in situations can you work on accepting and loving?

Remember the story of Ted? Loved back to health by his friends, Ted slowly gave up the pursuit of his "ideal self." Instead, he began to show people his real self with all its hurts, sinfulness, weakness, and immaturity. He didn't give up his pursuit of excellence; he put it in perspective. He learned that failure was not the end of the world and that success was not the basis of love. He loved his work, but he loved the people in his life even more. Therefore, he no longer needed the ideal (pp. 246–47).

God, thank you that in you and through your people I can find a place of "no condemnation." Teach me to extend the grace I find there to my real self. Help me replace the critical messages that I've internalized with words of your grace and truth.

Dear God, open my eyes to my badness and hear my confessions. Then help me to accept that badness as well as the truth that you accept me and love me anyway. Show me, too, where I need to extend the grace of forgiveness to others.

Help me to befriend the feelings of anger, sadness, and fear, to learn from them, and to let them keep me sensitive to others and to my need for you. Give me the courage to develop the other skills I need to integrate good and bad. Give me love for others when they are less than ideal and the ability to persevere in those relationships. And, as I learn to realistically expect badness and goodness in people, in the world, and in myself, help me to accept the bad graciously and celebrate the good joyfully. I pray in Jesus' name. Amen.

PART 4

Becoming *an* Adult

LESSON 11

What Is Adulthood?

Sara was one-down in all her important relationships. Working to gain acceptance and approval in order to feel that she was okay, she was not able to enjoy peer relationships with other adults. The freedom that adults have—to make their own decisions without permission from others, to evaluate and judge their own performance, to choose their own values and opinions, to disagree with others freely, and to enjoy sexual relations with an equal spouse—somehow had escaped her. Have these things escaped you, too? (pp. 251–52).

The Nature of the Problem

Becoming an adult is the process of moving out of a "one-up/one-down" relationship and into peer relationships with other adults. Becoming an adult is assuming the authority position of life, an important part of the image of God. We are all born children under adult authority, but over time we are to become authorities ourselves and be in charge of our lives (p. 252).

- Who was a good authority figure for you in the past? What did you appreciate about them? What kind of model do you want to emulate?

- What negative aspects of authority figures in your past do you disagree with and would like to be different from? Why did you not like these attributes and what sort of feelings did they create in you?

- Authority has a number of different facets. Consider where you have been given authority. In what areas do you have the power or right to give commands, enforce obedience, take action, or make final decisions?

- What expertise or knowledge gives you authority?

- What office or position of authority do you have?

- Where do you influence or affect people by what you do?

- Are you a positive or a negative authority figure to others? Support your answer.

- When do you give up your rights and serve others in submission?

- How do you feel as you live out the different aspects of your adulthood? Do you feel one-down to your contemporaries or do you defensively take the position of being one-up on everyone else?

The developmental task of establishing equality with other adults is imperative if guilt, anxiety, depression, sexual dysfunction, talent development, and spiritual servanthood are to be worked through. The process of starting as little people and becoming equal with big people involves gradually growing in stature and wisdom (Luke 2:52), to the point of being an equal-standing adult in an adult's world (p. 253).

- How do the tasks of bonding, having boundaries and separateness, and resolving good and bad help us reach this equal standing with other adults?

- Have you been well enough equipped by the first three tasks to deal with this fourth task of becoming an adult? How has the degree to which you have bonded, developed boundaries, and resolved good and bad affected the degree to which you have become an adult?

- Jesus calls us out of the one-down relationship to other people but encourages us to have respect for the role of authority at the same time (Matt. 23:2–5, 7–10). In what areas of your life do you submit to another's authority? How do you feel about that? Is it relatively easy or relatively difficult for you to submit to authority? Why?

People who see others as above them are still relating from a child's position of being under a person. We should think of other people as equal siblings under God, even if they have an office. To submit to them is to submit to God, not to people (pp. 253–54).

- How easy or difficult is it for you to submit to God? Why?
- Whose approval are you more concerned about, God's or other people's? Give evidence from your life to support your answer.
- When has your desire for the approval of other people interfered with your walk of faith (John 12:42–43)?

Both Jesus and Paul understood that to do the authoritative work of adulthood, one does not need permission on how one should think, feel, or act, nor should one be seeking the approval of other adults (Luke 6:26; John 5:44; 1 Thess. 2:4). This is what children do, and children cannot do the jobs of adults! That is, seeking the approval of God and not trying to please others is an important aspect of growing into adulthood. Adults are also accountable for the consequences of the things they do (pp. 255–56).

- Whom do you think of as a "take charge" person? What is attractive about him or her? How are you like that person?
- Whom do you think of as a wishy-washy person? What bothers you about him or her? How are you like that person?
- Would you describe yourself as more of a "take charge" or a wishy-washy person? In what situations are you more "take charge"? Why? When do you tend to be wishy-washy? Why?

The Biblical Basis for Authority

In the beginning, God made a glorious creation and entrusted it to human beings to govern and rule (Gen. 1:26, 28; 2:19). The one condition to this lofty position of authority was submission to a higher authority: God (Gen. 2:17). We have thus been given a lofty position of rulership and authority, of adulthood and responsibility, and of freedom to be "in charge" of our lives. Along with this comes the responsibility of submitting to God's authority and the accountability if we fail. Authority, responsibility, and accountability are three aspects of being "in charge" (pp. 256–57).

- What detrimental places and situations have you ended up in because you allowed some parent figure to run your life? Where have you fused with the ideas of someone else without thinking for yourself? Of whom have you been afraid to disagree with in your life? Where do you feel the consequences of your failure to take authority over the domain God has given you to manage?
- Where do you feel the consequences of being a slave, with sin having authority over you (Rom. 6:17–18)?

In God's plan of redemption, Christ was to get back what God lost and give it back to him, submitting to his authority (1 Cor. 15:22–28). Similarly, our redemption involves reversing the effects of the fall—returning, through Jesus, to the freedom and authority we had in the beginning (1 Cor. 15:45). Our Lord has given us the authority to take back what was lost, reclaim it, and give it back to him. That task is directly related to how much we walk in him (Col. 2:6; 3:3; 1 John 1:5–7; 2:4–6). To accomplish it we must do the two things Jesus did (pp. 257–61).

- Like Jesus, we must submit to authority and learn obedience (Heb. 5:7–8); and we must take authority over what is delegated to us, redeem what has been lost, and give it back to God. Rewrite this two-part assignment in the specifics of your own life. What authorities must you submit to and in what areas of your life must you take authority?

Jesus showed he had power to do things (Matt. 8:26–27; Mark 1:27); knowledge of God's Word and skill in interpreting it (Matt. 7:28–29); authority from the Father to be in his multifaceted position as Judge, Teacher, Savior, and Lord (John 5:26–27); influence with people gained by using his skills, knowledge, and talents for good (Mark 1:27); and the ability to give up his rights and to serve others in submission to God (Matt. 20:25–28; Phil. 2:5–8). Like Jesus and according to the example he sets for us, we are to grow up in these different aspects of authority. Jesus can help us become an authority over our lives (pp. 261–63).

A Developmental Perspective

If becoming an adult is a task that requires power and expertise, it is easy to see why it is so difficult. When we are born, we have very little of either. As we grow, however, we gain more ability and expertise through the processes of internalization and identification. As we internalize aspects of our parents and begin to identify with them as role models, we become like them (pp. 263–64).

The Early Years

The messages we learn and internalize in our youth greatly impact our attempt to become adults, and the first source of those empowering or immobilizing messages is our parents. In the beginning, the main internalization is love. Gradually, the aspects of authority—expertise, delegation, power, and accountability—increase (Luke 16:10). As we get older, sex-role typing and sexuality development take place. Then, as we internalize some of our parents' standards, performance becomes important. Between the ages of seven and twelve, mastery of tasks and work roles become important (pp. 264–65).

- Look back at your early years. What does the developmental overview outlined above help you understand about yourself? What positive things have you internalized? What negative messages have you internalized?

The Role of Parents

While children are growing and developing the power, expertise, and influence they need for adulthood, parents can help or harm their identification with each aspect of authority. If children hate the source of these dimensions of authority, they will have a difficult time both developing their own authority and later submitting to God's (pp. 265–70).

Power—If the nature of a parent's power is gentle, warm, and loving, as well as firm, the child will sense that personal power is a good thing. If a parent exercises power either passively or harshly, the child will get a mixed-up notion of power (pp. 265–67).

- Think back to age twelve or thirteen. What was your idea of power? Where did it come from? How did your parents exercise their power? Were they passive and domineering, or did they have a good sense of personal power? How did your parents exasperate or discourage you (Eph. 6:1–4; Col. 3:20–21)?

Expertise—While growing up, children should have ample opportunity to acquire more and more expertise. Parents should model expertise themselves as well as support the process in their children. If children have the opportunity to learn that they can learn, the rest of life is a cinch. They develop a basic belief in their ability to tackle any task (pp. 267–68).

- In what areas did your parents model expertise? What were you interested in learning about as you were growing up? How did they support your acquisition of knowledge and expertise? What resources and opportunities did they make available?
- How did your parents discourage your acquisition of knowledge and expertise? When did they say no to resources and opportunities you were interested in? What talents have you neglected developing? Why?

Correction—Good parenting follows the example of our High Priest, Jesus, who corrects gently, for he empathizes with our weakness (Heb. 4:15–5:2). Good parenting, like

God himself, models for us a loving and accepting relationship between the ideal and the real that encourages our growth (pp. 268–69).

- What kind of relationship between the ideal and the real did your parents model? How did they respond to your failures? How did they respond when you tried new things? What attitude toward failure and trying new things have you developed?

The Power of the Office—Developing respect for the office of parent lays a basis for a child's later respect for the law, governing authorities, and church authorities (Rom. 13:1). Therefore children need parent figures who are authoritative and who possess the power of their office of parent (pp. 269–70).

- How did your parents handle the office of parent? How much respect did you have for them because they held that office? What did they do to earn this respect or lose your respect? How does your attitude toward other offices (police, government officials, church leaders) compare to your attitude toward your parents?

Adolescence

If these developmental processes go well, the stage is set for a healthy twelve-year-old to go crazy. During adolescence a little person is becoming a big person, trying to take power over his or her life, and stepping into the adult world in an equal role while not quite there. The child, or near-adult, has one foot in each camp. Adolescence is the beginning of undoing the yoke of slavery called childhood (Gal. 4:1–5). Like every other overthrow of government, it usually doesn't happen without rebellion (pp. 270–74).

- What was your adolescence like? What do you remember thinking, feeling, wanting, worrying about, and dreaming about? Or have you even entered adolescence?

If not, why have you resisted becoming an adult, and who has helped you resist by playing god in your life?

- What forms did your rebellion against parental control take? How did your parents respond?
- How did you respond to parental influence? What other authority figures influenced you during your adolescence? What extracurricular activities were you involved in? What role did they play in your movement toward adulthood?
- What kind of peer group did you find yourself fitting into? Was theirs a positive or negative influence? How did you deal with your emerging sexuality? And how did your parents? Have you come into your own sexual identity since adolescence or are you still "hush, hush" about sex?
- What happened to your faith during your adolescent years? What values did you question and discard (Luke 15:11–24)? What values did you question and then claim as your own? Which of your parents' standards did you discard? What did you replace them with?

If the questioning and learning of adolescence goes well, the people who come out the other end can be called adults. They are their own person, responsible for themselves; they leave home, establish a life of their own with their own talents, direction, purpose, power, office, influence, and expertise, and have a good beginning in healthy submission. They no longer look to other adults to perform parental functions for them (such as thinking for them or telling them what to believe and how to live). Other adults are looked to as experts who can offer advice and input, but each person is responsible for his or her own life (pp. 273–74).

- Summarize now what your parents taught you about authority. What were their strengths and weaknesses? What were the strengths and weaknesses of other authority figures from early in your life?
- How did your parents injure you, and have you forgiven them? Why not? What is the block?

The Spiritual Implications of the Adolescent Passage

The adolescent passage is when we overthrow the legalistic structures that interfere with our relationship with God. We need to chisel away at the authority of our parents as godlike figures so that God can be our parent. In short, we need to put aside our parents so that we can be adopted by God. If we never put aside our parents, we will suffer from spiritual childhood and not be able to get out from under the law and the slavery of rules (p. 274).

- What "elemental spiritual forces of the world" (Gal. 4:3) or rules of religion have authority over you today? On what points are you legalistic about the way you live out the Christian faith? In what ways are you always trying to be "good enough" in your faith?
- Whose freedom do you try to take away by being legalistic and putting rules on them? To whom do you need to apologize for this?

Paul teaches that we are to be freed from the rules and adopted as sons and daughters of God (Gal. 4:1–7). This freedom from parental structures leads us to a love relationship with God and an obedience to his principles of love (pp. 274–75).

- How do you feel threatened by this freedom to live according to principles that grow out of a love-based way of thinking rather than according to black-and-white rules? What is appealing about it? Why?
- Where do you, like the Pharisees, follow blindly "the tradition of the elders" (Mark 7:5) and think it more important to please parent figures than to please God (Luke 11:47–48)? Do you feel more comfortable hiding behind strict legalistic formulas?
- What authority figures did you falsely comply with after you were old enough not to do so? Why? What legalists have you succumbed to? Why?
- When did you, like Jesus (Luke 2:49; John 2:4) and unlike the Pharisees (Mark 7:1–8), assert your independence from your parents' faith and make it your own?

When did you begin to live out your faith by making decisions in light of love (1 Cor. 13:11–13)?

Like Jesus, we need to come out from under our parents' authority and give our allegiance to God. When this happens, our thinking shifts from black-and-white rules to principles interpreted in light of love. As spiritual adolescents, we find ourselves clinging much more closely to God, our Father, for we need his direction through the fog that comes when we discover that our theology does not have an answer for every situation. At that time, we find ourselves needing a relationship with him, not just a system of rules (pp. 275–79).

- When have you tried to submit to God's will in the midst of pain (Luke 22:42)? Did this prompt your spiritual adolescence and a questioning of your faith? If so, what did you learn? Or did you cling to the traditions of your elders and not let yourself deal with life's hard questions? Why? What is keeping you from entering your spiritual adolescence now?

It takes someone who feels equal to other adults to be able to do the things God asks us to do. We must own our lives and not need parental approval so that we "are not trying to please people but God, who tests our hearts" (1 Thess. 2:4). The next lesson looks at what happens when we don't (p. 280).

Again, God, I am understanding more and more about why I am the way I am and about the kind of person you want me to be—free to be in relationship to you and free to live according to principles of love. And I see where I still feel and act like a little person in a big person's world.

God, please help me grow up where I need to grow up and to redeem the wrong ideas I have about authority that are rooted in my childhood and adolescence. Replace them with a right understanding that comes from the way you deal with power, expertise, correction, the power of office, and submission.

May I learn to seek your approval rather than the approval of other people. Give me the courage to rebel so that my faith can become my own and I can become your child. Give me the courage I need to live in freedom and in a love relationship with you. I pray in Jesus' name. Amen.

LESSON 12

When We Fail to Grow Up

Remember the observation that "we should be adults first and then children. It's too hard the other way around"? The task of becoming adults certainly is a difficult task to leave to children (p. 281)!

Symptoms of an Inability to Become an Adult

Everyone who has ever lived (except Adam and Eve) has encountered the problem of being born a little person in a big person's world and being given the task of becoming a big person over time. This task is not easy, and some people never accomplish it. The text discusses twenty-two problems that can arise when we have not yet taken charge of our lives and are trying to live adulthood from the one-down child position (pp. 281–93).

- As you read through the list of problems below, check the box next to any you've encountered. Then write down any words or phrases from the text that describe your experience and help you better understand what is going on in your life.
- What has this list of problems shown you about yourself? Have you been trying to manage symptoms (inordinate need for approval, fear of disapproval, feelings of

inferiority, hate for authority figures, etc.) rather than dealing with the root of the problem—the inability to achieve adulthood?

Barriers to Becoming an Adult

Now that you understand how you have not yet become an adult, consider what distorted convictions—about yourself, others, God, and the world—have stagnated you. These distortions need to be challenged and risked in relationships (pp. 293–95).

- Place a check mark next to any of the following ideas that have taken up residence in your heart and mind.
  - "I am bad if others don't approve of me; their disapproval proves it!"
  - "I am less than others."
  - "I must please others to be liked."
  - "I am bad if I disagree."
  - "My opinions are not as good as those of others."
  - "I have no right to my own opinions."
  - "I must get permission from others to . . ."
  - "I am bad if I fail."
  - "I shouldn't feel so sexual."
  - "Sexual feelings are bad."
  - "My plans will never succeed."
  - "I should defer to their beliefs, even though I disagree."
  - "I need someone else to manage my life; I am not capable enough."
  - "If I differ, I am wrong."
  - "I think they should . . ."
  - "I shouldn't let myself feel . . ."
  - "I am better than they are."
  - "My group is the right group."
  - "We really have the best theology."

- "Our ministry is the only real one."
- "I know what's best for them."
- "I know better than they do."
- "I could never teach him or her anything."
- "Adulthood is out of my grasp."
- "Other people are all disapproving and critical."
- "They are better than me."
- "They will like me better if I am compliant."
- "They think that I am wrong or bad for disagreeing."
- "Their opinions are always right."
- "They will think I am bad for failing."
- "They have no weaknesses."
- "They never fail like I do."
- ". . . is easy for them."
- "Their beliefs are better than mine."
- "They know what's best for me."
- "They never feel . . ."
- "They know everything."
- "They are never this afraid, or mad, or sad, or . . ."
- "They will hate me for standing up to them."
- "God likes for me to be nice to everyone."
- "God wants me to always defer to my authorities, never questioning."
- "God does not want me to run my own life. He wants my 'leaders' to do that."
- "God disapproves of me when I fail, just as my parents disapproved."
- "God does not like me to be aggressive."
- "God does not like me to disagree with the pastor."
- "God thinks others are more (or less) important than me."
- "God does not allow me freedom to choose some of my own values. They are all prescribed in the Bible. There are no gray areas."
- "God wants me to adhere to a bunch of rules."

- ⊚ "God likes discipline and sacrifice more than compassion, love, and relationships."
- ⊚ "Competition is bad; someone always gets hurt."
- ⊚ "Disagreement is bad; someone always gets hurt."
- ⊚ "Conflict is bad; someone always loses."
- ⊚ "There is no such thing as a 'win-win' relationship."
- ⊚ "People who are people-pleasers are liked better than people who say what they think."
- ⊚ "Everything has a 'right answer'—especially since we have the Bible."
- ⊚ "There is a right way and a wrong way of seeing everything. Perspective makes no difference."
- ⊚ "Flexibility is license and lawlessness."
- ⊚ "Sexuality is evil."
- ⊚ "There is a right way and a wrong way to do everything."
- ⊚ "It will never work."
- What experiences gave you these distortions?
- What are you doing to counter these experiences and the resulting distortions? What truths can you now cite to respond to your inaccurate ideas?

These heartfelt but misguided convictions about self, others, God, and the world are barriers to becoming an adult. But they are barriers that can be overcome with work, risk, prayer, relationship, and practice (p. 295).

Becoming an Adult

Before learning more in the next chapter about how to overcome distorted thinking and unwholesome behavior that keeps you from becoming an adult, take a prayerful inventory to see where you are feeling like a little person in a big person's world.

- With whom do you feel one-down right now? In what areas? Why? Is it a good one-down (as in mentoring) or is it a bad one-down (as in feeling like less of a person)?

- With whom are you trying to be one-up? Why? Do you realize that you are play-ing God in that person's life?

- Whom are you trying to please? Whose approval are you trying to earn? Why? Is it worth it? Has earning people's approval been a pattern in your life? Has that effort ever helped you?

- What talents and expertise are you not developing at present because of some sort of fear? What are you doing about that fear? Are you getting help? How can you step out in faith to develop that expertise and allow God to make you into an adult?

- What role or office do you resist identifying with because of conflict? Why?

- What authority figures in your life (your boss, the police, your board of elders, God, the IRS) are you failing to submit to lovingly? How can this be destructive?

- What authority figures do you feel anger and hatred toward? What are you doing with those feelings? Make sure that you do not deny them, but also don't fail to resolve them.

- With whom are you currently fusing in terms of thoughts and opinions rather than stating your own? With whom are you afraid to disagree? Why?

- In what situations do you hide from your sexual feelings or thoughts? Why? Who is the parent figure there?

- What "spiritual" group do you act "nice" around? What group of your friends are more adolescent? Why are you trying to please this "spiritual" group and then passively rebelling on the side? How is this practice keeping you a child?

- Which person in your life are you most afraid of being judged by? Why?

- What doubts do you have about God or theology that you are afraid to face and research on your own? What is keeping you from finding out what you believe?

- With which current spiritual leaders do you disagree? To whom are you afraid to express your thoughts? Why?

- How are your spouse or closest friends functioning as parent figures in the nega-tive sense of the term?

God, I have a lot of growing up to do before I can really live as your child. I am realizing the freedom that I miss and the difficulties that arise when I try to live adulthood from a one-down child position. I ask that, with the guidance of your Spirit, you would enable me to grow up in my thinking, in my behavior, and in my faith. Some of those problems that have arisen because I have not yet become an adult are now long-held patterns. God, please uproot them that I may know freedom in your love and equality in the world of adults.

And, as I've asked before, I again ask that the light of your truth would clarify and correct my distorted thinking about myself, about other people, about you, and about the world—thoughts that block my becoming an adult who lives in submission to you and you alone. Enable me, too, to grow up in my faith, in order that I may thrive in relationship to you and live according to the principle of your love. In Jesus' name. Amen.

LESSON 13

Learning to Become
Mature Adults

Learning to become an adult is not an easy task. Perhaps becoming an adult while you are already living in an adult body is even harder, but it is necessary if you want to get out from under the authority of others. In this lesson we will look at some of the skills you need to become your own master under God, to become a mature adult (p. 296).

Reevaluate Beliefs

We need to follow the example of the apostle Paul, who took "captive every thought to make it obedient to Christ" (2 Cor. 10:5), and reevaluate what we believe. The time is past for "inherited beliefs"; it is time for an adult faith (p. 297).

- Why do you believe what you believe—because you really believe it or because someone told you to believe it? What will be your first step toward taking an inventory of your faith? Whom will you turn to when questions arise?

Disagree with Authority Figures

Life has many gray areas, and an adult does not hesitate to disagree with other adults. Be honest about your disagreements with others (p. 297).

- Where are you following the pack in your thinking rather than having your own ideas or being open about your disagreement? Where are you forcing an issue to be black or white and ignoring the gray?
- Remember that when we disagree we are iron sharpening iron (Prov. 27:17). What ideas will you stop fearing to voice and think about? When will you voice them? To whom?
- Whom will you begin to show your real thoughts to? When will you next see that person?

See Parents and Authority Figures Realistically

Knock parents and other authority figures off the pedestal you've put them on. See their weaknesses as well as their strengths (pp. 297–98).

- With whom do you agree on everything? Who do you think has it all together? Now look at those people closely. What weaknesses do you see? Where do you disagree with what they believe and think?
- What mistakes do you see that your parents have made? What sins have they committed? Identify their mistakes and forgive them.

Make Your Own Decisions

If people in your life are telling you what to think, believe, do, or buy, start making those decisions yourself. Learn to think and act for yourself (p. 298).

- Who are you letting play the role of parent in your life and thereby take away your freedom as God's child (Gal. 4:8–9)? Why?
- What will you do the next time you hear "you should"?

Practice Disagreeing

Practice what you could not do as you were growing up: Disagree with and do not do what self-appointed human "gods" are telling you to do. Learn how to say, "I see your point, but I look at it differently. I think . . ." (pp. 298–99).

- Which authority figure do you need to go to and disagree with? When will you do that?

Deal with Your Sexuality

If you are prudish or embarrassed by sex, work on reeducating yourself about its beauty; desensitize yourself to a "no-no" attitude toward sex (p. 299).

- How will you get in touch with your adult sexual role? When will you take the first step? What will you do to become more aware of your sexual feelings? When will you take the first step?

Give Yourself Permission to Be Equal with Your Parents

Many authority problems have as their kernel the inability to assume the role held by the same-sex parent. Appreciate where your parent succeeded and choose other role models for where he or she failed (pp. 299–300).

- Think about the role you saw your same-sex parent play. Did you dislike the way he or she functioned in that role? If so, be specific. Or were you afraid of taking the role over? What do you think you could do to usurp his or her position?
- Whether you disliked the way your same-sex parent functioned or were afraid of taking over the role, now look at the way that parent succeeded in his or her role. What can you learn? Find other role models for where your father or mother failed.

Recognize and Pursue Talents

To become an adult requires that you own and recognize the talents and gifts God has given you (p. 300).

- What talents have you buried in the ground? What plans will you make to develop your expertise and be a good steward of the gifts God has given you? What is the first step you will take, and when will you take it?
- If you don't know what talents and gifts God has given you, ask him to show you. Also, get some other people's insight. Whom will you ask? When?

Practice

As with any skill, we need to practice becoming an adult. You must also give yourself permission to fail (pp. 300–301).

- What role will you do better at assuming authority over? What will you do today to begin?
- What person will you do better at assuming authority over? How will you start?
- Whom will you stop "obeying" that you have no business obeying?
- What person will you stop hiding from? When will you take the first step?

Recognize the Privileges of Adulthood

As Paul says in Galatians 4:1, the child owns everything, but is not free to use it. But adults are. You have the freedom to choose for yourself (p. 301).

- What choice will you make in each of the following categories to start owning and using the privileges God has given adults?
  - Talents
  - Values
  - Beliefs
  - Relationship with God
  - Tastes
  - Friends
  - Church
  - Other

Discipline Yourself

Adults do what ants do: They take responsibility for their tasks without waiting for a superior to instruct them (Prov. 6:6–8) (p. 301).

- In what areas of your life could you afford to be more disciplined? Choose one area and decide what you are going to do about your lack of discipline. Find someone who will hold you accountable, and then take the first step.

Gain Authority Over Evil

The Bible commands us to "resist the devil, and he will flee from you" (James 4:7). The Word of God and the power of Jesus' name are sufficient for you to bind the forces of evil (pp. 301–2).

- How do you exercise your authority, given to you by Christ, over evil? What do you need to learn about spiritual warfare? Where will you learn it?

Submit to Others Out of Freedom

An important aspect of becoming an adult is learning to submit to others in love, without an authority conflict (see Matt. 5:39; Rom. 13:1; Eph. 5:21; Heb. 13:17; James 4:7; 1 Peter 2:18–19) (p. 302).

- Whom are you not now submitting to that you can submit to in love rather than compliance? When and how will you start?

Do Good Works

In Ephesians 2:10, Paul writes, "We are God's handiwork, created in Christ Jesus to do good works." You are a prized possession and have been given a task to perform for the Lord (p. 302).

- What good works has God called you to do for him? Where are you responding to his call now? If you are in a building and healing time, are you using this period to listen for God's call?

Become a "Pharisee Buster"

We all have remnants of legalistic thinking and remain to some degree under the tutor of parental approval (pp. 302–3).

- How are you still operating under the old system of gaining the approval of others in order to be okay? Be specific.
- Where has legalism crept into your faith? What will you do to stop trying to earn approval?

Appreciate Mystery and the Unknown

One of the hallmarks of people with authority problems is their inability to tolerate mystery and the unknown. They need an answer for everything.

- Where do you have God in a box? What questions do you refuse to ask because the answers may not be black and white? What situations or settings remind you that God is unsearchable (Rom. 11:33–34)? Meditate on those and let them serve as a call to worship.

Love and Appreciate People Who Are Different

People often see other people as not as good because they are still trying to be the better child (p. 303).

- What siblings (real siblings or siblings in the Lord) do you need to stop competing with? What will you do to learn that different does not necessarily mean superior/inferior? What siblings will you stop treating as if they were your parents? What siblings do you need to stop parenting?
- What verses from Scripture will you memorize to help you remember that you cannot earn God's love but can rest in his gracious unconditional love for you? As examples, see John 3:16; Romans 5:8; 1 Peter 3:18; and 1 John 3:16.

Remember the story of Sara? When she began to understand her background and realize that she had never been allowed or encouraged to become an adult, she went to work. Growing up took a lot of time, prayer, and effort, but in the end Sara won. Out of a forty-year-old little girl, God grew an adult—and he can do the same for you (pp. 303–6).

God, thank you for the hope I find in you—in your unconditional love, healing power, and redemptive work—and the hope I find in these steps I can take toward becoming an adult. Please give me the courage I need to take these steps.

Be with me, I ask, as I learn to disagree with authority figures, make my own decisions, pursue my talents, and discipline myself. Give me a realistic view of my parents and other authority figures and enable me to finally see myself as an adult who is my parents' equal. May I come to enjoy my sexuality, the privileges of adulthood, and people who are different from me. I look forward, Lord, to the satisfaction of doing the good works you call me to. Help me hear your call.

Finally, teach me to submit to you, who are indeed unfathomable in your greatness and glory. I pray in Jesus' name. Amen.

Conclusion

Each section of the book begins with the story of a Christian struggling with bonding, setting boundaries, sorting out issues of good and bad, or becoming an adult (p. 307).

- What have you learned about your own struggle in each of these areas? Below, write down the two or three greatest barriers you face as you work on completing the task. Also note two or three steps you have taken toward overcoming those barriers and completing each task since you began this study.
  - Bonding
  - Setting boundaries
  - Sorting out issues of good and bad
  - Becoming an adult

Besides explaining these four tasks, this study intended to make five other points clear. First, we all struggle with all four issues (p. 307).

- What does this fact mean to you? How is it encouraging? Whom have you found to support you in your struggle and to share his or her own struggles?

Second, there is no such thing as either an emotional problem or a spiritual problem. Because of our broken relationships with God, others, and ourselves, we develop symptoms that we feel on an emotional level and live out in our spiritual lives (p. 307).

- How have you lived out your emotional pain in your spiritual life? Where in your life have you seen the connection between these two? Be specific.
- Where are you experiencing the healing power of love—God's love and the love of other people? If you aren't yet doing so, ask God to bring into your life someone who will support you or ask him to give you the courage to build a relationship with people who are already available to you.

Third, our symptoms are not the problems. Healing is only superficial when we focus on the symptoms rather than the problems (pp. 307–8).

- What symptoms did *Changes That Heal* help you recognize? What issues have those symptoms caused you to confront?
- What specific steps are you taking to deal with the issues behind those symptoms? Be specific.

Fourth, meaning, purpose, satisfaction, and fulfillment are fruits of the four tasks we've been looking at. Meaning comes from love, which flows out of bonding. Purpose comes from direction and truth, which form boundaries. Satisfaction comes from having the less than perfect be "good enough" in light of God's ideal, and fulfillment comes from the adult ability to exercise talents (p. 308).

- Where are you now experiencing these four fruits? Explain how working on each task is enabling you to experience the corresponding fruit.
  - *Meaning*—from bonding
  - *Purpose*—from forming boundaries
  - *Satisfaction*—from accepting the less than perfect as good enough
  - *Fulfillment*—from exercising your talents as an adult

Finally, "the greatest of these is love" (1 Cor. 13:13). The model set forth in this book can help us become functioning human beings; but if that is the final goal, we have sold ourselves short. We were made to love, and the fully functioning person is one who takes his bonded, separate, forgiving, adult self into the world and denies that self for the sake of others (p. 308).

- Summarize what you have learned about love in this study. What new insights have you gained? What new ways are you thinking and acting as a result?
- How does the fact of God's unconditional and eternal love for you encourage you to continue working on bonding with him and with other people, setting boundaries, resolving the issues of good and bad, and becoming an adult?
- Where are you serving and acting as God's agent to a hurting world? What new plans are you developing that share his love and healing with others?

As you close this book, resolve to keep working. Work on your ability to attach to others so that you can have your empty heart filled. Work on setting boundaries so you can own your own life. Work on confessing and receiving forgiveness so you can develop your real personhood. Work on assuming adulthood so you can be an authority. Then, go out and give it to others. Remember, "Greater love has no one than this: to lay down one's life for one's friends" (John 15:13). God bless you.

CHURCHES
THAT — HEAL

by DR. HENRY CLOUD

HELPING THE CHURCH BECOME A
PLACE HURTING PEOPLE RUN TO,
NOT AWAY FROM

ChurchesThatHeal.com

Churches That Heal is an all-new, digital resource designed to equip pastors and churches to handle issues of mental and emotional health in their communities through a biblical and psychologically sound plan of healing. Through over 40 videos and digital downloads on the *Churches That Heal* platform, leaders will learn about the processes for healing that God outlines in Scripture, be given practical solutions for meeting the needs of those struggling in their communities, and experience healing themselves.

Learn more at ChurchesThatHeal.com